Anne Elizabeth

I'm a
Registered
Dietitian...

Now What?

I'm a Registered Dietitian...

Now What?

Anne Elizabeth

www.anneelizabethrd.com

For my tribe

Table of Contents

Table of Contents

Prelude

I don't want to look back and think, I could have eaten that.

- Anonymous

No one told me the wild ride I would have becoming a registered dietitian.

No one told me what to expect when applying for internships. No one told me to get exposure to the profession and make experiences happen to better understand the profession. No one told me how to find my first job. No one told me how being a registered dietitian can be exciting and rewarding. No one told me it can be heartbreaking. No one told me about all the different aspects of our profession and all the different things I could do and be. No one told me my first job did not need to be my last job.

There was so much that no one told me.

That is why I am writing this. Being a registered dietitian is a journey. One that is unique for every one of us but also one that is very much the same. Consider it similar to a recipe you are creating: full of different ingredients that hopefully leads to a particular delicious and satisfying outcome with a few tweaks along the way. This book will hopefully help you create and recreate your recipe along your registered dietitian journey and find you right where you are. As registered dietitians, or what I like to call "my tribe," we need to build each other up and help each other along the way.

I want to share my ideas, thoughts and musings I have experienced so far in my journey. I want to be your confidant, your therapist and your biggest cheerleader along your journey. I want this book to be something you read at different stages and times in your profession. I want you to know you are not alone.

I know this may sound a little quirky, but I would have done anything for a mentor to help me along my journey to provide guidance, support, conversations about this kooky registered dietitian world and to explore ways to keep growing. I really didn't know I needed a one or what I was looking for in a mentor. Now I know this and so much more. I also know I am not even close to being done learning yet. Nutrition is a field that is always going to be in a state of flux and I aim to change with it the best way I can. Along the way, I have had much professional growth and personal growth. I have also had setbacks and times when I felt time was standing still. It is never too early or late to create a blueprint that makes you happy and fulfilled.

I want you to see you have a purpose in this profession and it will come from the passion you have, the reason why you became a registered dietitian. I want you to feel, encompass and embody the greatness of being the real nutrition expert.

There is no greater power than knowing there are others sharing in a similar journey.

Please share this with other registered dietitians wherever they are in their journey and with the new frontier of RD's-to-be so together, we can eliminate the "no-ones" in our profession and replace it with names and faces. Let's make this the best damn journey we possibly can. While reading this, be open to doing a little work and a little soul searching. Be ready to laugh, learn, answer tough questions and be extremely excited, hopeful, and open for all there is just waiting for you as a registered dietitian.

Your profession is not what brings home your weekly paycheck, your profession is what you're put here on earth to do, with such passion and such intensity that it becomes spiritual in calling.

- Vincent Van Gogh, Dutch Post-Impressionist painter.

Introduction

Cauliflower is nothing but cabbage with a college education.
- Mark Twain, American author and humorist.

HOLY SH*%! YOU HAVE DONE IT!

Congratulations! You survived organic chemistry, (I still can't believe I survived that class). You did not burn, blow up or ruin anything in foods class. You learned to calculate a variety of tube feedings and TPN's. You figured out you never want to be a biochemist or microbiologist, and you found every volunteer opportunity to pad your internship application with experience.

You bravely and nervously started the application process for your internship. You wrote, rewrote and wrote again your personal statement and resume and meticulously reviewed the perfection of your application. You trusted professionals along the way to write letters of recommendations praising you as the future of dietetics. Finally, you submitted your applications for your internship after many hours of research and consideration of which ones would fit you the best.

Hellloooo, match day. Seriously, how nuts (bat-sh*% crazy nuts) did you feel in anticipation of this day? I bet you can still recall the feeling you had when you went online (or in my case, waiting frantically for the Fed-Ex guy to arrive) to discover your destiny. And then, in one of the most breathless moments in your life, you discover.....YOU WERE MATCHED! You were accepted into an internship, you were on your way to becoming a registered dietitian. You gladly paid an institution to gain hands-on dietetic experience (also known as working for free) in this rewarding field.

Throughout the months or years of your internship, you found your groove and realized (or thought you did) what kind of dietitian you wanted to be when you grew up. You weathered through all the extra assignments you had to complete after each exhausting day. You fought back fears, put on your "I know exactly what I am doing hat" to conquer the unknown during each "staff relief" week you were assigned. You made connections with multiple preceptors you were privileged to work with and have a vast variety of "colorful" clientele whose stories will forever hold a special place in your intern heart.

There were times you did not know everything. You realized a lot of what you learned in your classes, and how you learned to do them, were not at all what it was like in the practicing world. You were exposed to things you did not learn in class and you made notes, lots of notes (I still have my notes). Then there were the late nights while doing assignments, you may have questioned why you wanted to be a registered dietitian. Remember when you were so tired you could barely keep your eyes open or prevent them from filling up with tears and knew you still had 5 hours worth of assignments to do after a 10-hour day at the hospital?

YOU MADE IT! You made it through tray line and a 50-page chart on a complicated patient. You made it through recipe analysis and your first newly diagnosed diabetic education. Looking back, I hope you see how special this time was in your life and how this experience is something no one can take away from you, but many people relate to.

You made it through your RD exam. Sitting there, facing the computer and answering each question, not knowing when the questions would stop and the screen would go blank. You sat patiently and full of hope, staring at the screen, waiting to see the message pop up that you passed. YOU PASSED!

Right there, at that moment, you became a Registered Dietitian. All your hard work. All your dedication. All your passion for food, health and helping people navigate through this crazy world of nutrition began at that very moment when "Congratulations!" came across the screen. You feel the excitement of what lies ahead. You cannot wait to get out there and share all the knowledge you have absorbed through this process. You are ready to conquer the world and be the nutrition expert. You leave the testing center with a huge smile on your face. You feel confident and satisfied with all your hard work. You sit back, taking a moment to reflect on your achievement, and then reality sets in.

I'm a Registered Dietitian. Now What?

Your time is limited, so don't waste it living someone else's life. Don't be trapped by dogma-which is living with the results of other people's thinking. Don't let the noise of other's' opinions drown out your inner voice. And most important, have the courage to follow your heart and intuition. They somehow already know what you truly want to become. Everything else is secondary.

- Steve Jobs, American information technology entrepreneur and inventor.

Part One:

Get Ready.
Set?
Go!

You don't have to be great to start,
but you have to start to be great.

One

Your Story, Your Journey, Your Passion

Cooking is like love, it should be entered into abandon or not at all.
- Harriet Van Horne; American newspaper columnist and
film/television critic.

My Story

It was the spring semester of my sophomore year in college. It was time to register for my classes for my fall semester and junior year. I was Pre-Med with a Biology major and was perfectly on track with all my classes to prepare me for medical school. Unfortunately, I was not gifted with the brain for science (and come to think about it, math, philosophy and history, either, sigh). All the aptitude tests I took told me to avoid the sciences.

But my passion and my interests were consumed by science. When I was in grade school and middle school, all I could dream about was being a doctor. When I was in high school, I was focused on going to Creighton University because of its reputation for medicine. I had to work really hard to do well in my classes. I mean really really really hard. I hired tutors and spent many very late nights of studying in the good old Reinhart Library. There were many failed chemistry lab lessons, many study groups and meetings with professors to make sure I was understanding the material.

Being a student was a full-time job and studying was my part-time job. I managed to survive and complete 2 years of science and core classes, I finally had time to take an elective class this particular semester. Electives seemed like a far off fantasy land I only heard stories about. As I scanned the course catalog, Aerobics, Creative Writing and Nutrition were at the top of my list. I had a brief moment of weakness and really wanted to work on my fitness, so aerobics was calling my name.

Realistically, since I had my eyes on the prize and wanted to graduate in four years, I chose to be as professionally driven as possible making Nutrition for Health Careers the better choice. A doctor needs to have some nutritional knowledge for their patients, right? (Can't help taking a brief moment to realize how funny is this, knowing what I know now about nutrition education for physicians). I registered and was all set to conquer advanced biology classes, study for the MCAT and finally enjoy an elective class.

Nutrition for Health Careers was a class formulated for nursing and allied health students at my university. Nursing students and allied health students were very different from pre-med majors. They had all been in class together from day one and knew each other very well. I was an oddly colored and shaped fish out of water in this class (and I did not wear scrubs or a lab coat) but knew I really needed to be "all-in" for my future physician career.

Even though I felt a little out of place in the class of mostly nursing students, the class felt very comfortable from day one. For me, the first day of any new class brought anxiety as soon as the syllabus was handed out. Shockingly, it wasn't the case in this one. A registered dietitian taught the class and I found myself always looking forward to her class. I never once thought about skipping class (Sorry Dad and Mom, I am guilty of maybe doing this a few times!) because I was mesmerized by every lecture and found myself wanting to know more. The day we talked about macronutrients, I still remember being shocked water was considered one. And I thought I was well versed in the biological sciences? I was mesmerized by the lectures on vitamins and minerals and the role they played in simple chemical functions within our bodies.

This particular lecture made me forever grateful to my Mom for setting out a MVI each morning with my breakfast during my adolescence and how she planned each meal to have a portion of each of the food groups. I was realizing the connection I had to nutrition at a young age and everything in this class was exciting, had me wanting more and shockingly, came easy for me. The tests and assignments did not require me to study long hours, hire a tutor, or spend endless hours in the professor's office because it just clicked. It all made sense in my jumbled-up biology brain. I found myself easily doing well in the class and it was such a breath of fresh air. Ahhhhhh! This was the perfect class to help prepare me for med school and to regain some collegiate confidence.

Halfway through the semester, our professor lectured on the healthcare team in a professional setting and she discussed what being a registered dietitian was. As I sat in class this day, it seriously was like someone smacked me upside the head and said, Anne, you should be a registered dietitian! A whirlwind of thoughts went through my head.

I love this material. I love the thought of how we can prevent disease and maintain health through good and balanced nutrition. I am excited how there is a role for registered dietitians on a healthcare team and when someone is sick or hospitalized, nutrition plays an important part in their recovery. I am honestly excited that carrots really do help your vision because of vitamin A. Adequate protein intake can help your wounds heal faster. I do not get 25 grams of fiber a day! And don't even get me started on my water intake.

One night after studying for yet another Biology exam, I decided to look into what it takes to be a registered dietitian. It was late, past midnight, and I started to surf the internet on schooling for registered dietitians. I quickly discovered this was not a major my current university offered. We had a few nutrition classes offered at my school, but to become a registered dietitian, you needed to have a degree in dietetics and nutrition or be able to take the necessary classes to qualify for an internship. An internship, wait. What? I started to feel a little overwhelmed and tad bit defeated.

After further research, I quickly discovered a degree was not enough and I would have to apply and be accepted into an internship program and take a national exam. Hmmm, sounded a lot like medical school. Since I was not attending a university with this program, I had to find which ones did offer the degree. There was one in the same city in which I was currently residing. I quickly found the information online and what classes I needed to qualify for an internship.

After discovering what I have been taking was all very similar to what a registered dietitian needed, I was hopeful it would be an easy transition. I finished out my junior year and at the start of my senior year, I met with an advisor at an approved dietetic program and realized I would need to take a "few" classes over a span of 4 more semesters. Yep, you heard it, 2 more years of undergrad. Ugh. I was not too keen on more schooling and 4 semesters seemed exhausting. Only because I was comparing it to my last 4 semesters.

As bewildered as I was, I could not get it off my mind and something was truly calling me to do this. Over a span of two weeks, I had undeniable aching in my mind and heart for this as my future profession. It knew it was time to talk things over with Dad and Mom. I remember sitting at their kitchen table and saying,

Ok, so I have something I want to discuss with you. I am thinking about changing my life plan professionally and it is going to require me to go to college just a wee bit longer (cue eye batting and sweet adorable smile).

With two extremely blank faces staring back at me, I then told them the part about 2 more years and an internship and a test. Absolutely relieved, my parents were nothing but supportive and only wanted the best for me. They helped me sort out the best plan with my current school and my future school. I stayed devoted to graduating with my Biology degree from Creighton, set up the next two years and map out my didactic plan to become what I know I was destined to and really wanted to be when I grew up:

A Registered Dietitian.

My next 2 years proved to be exactly the right decision. I loved every one of my classes. I excelled in every one of my classes. It was great being surrounded by other students who felt the same way I did. My mind, my heart and my passion was for nutrition. It was all confirmation I was meant to be a registered dietitian. I was flourishing, excited about the future and actually felt like I knew what the hell I was doing! After I finished my didactic program with the University of Nebraska-Omaha, I applied for and landed an internship with Iowa State University. I was finally on my way to the job of my dreams.

This is my story. My story of how I made the decision to be a registered dietitian. It is nothing glamorous and I feel it might have not been an actual decision but a calling. All I know is I did make the decision to take the nutrition class when I was pre-med and I am pretty sure the rest happened because it truly was the calling that finally called.

Maybe for you it has been one year or 30 years, but I think it is important to always go back to why you wanted to be a registered dietitian. Just by writing the above story, I had the same feelings racing through me when I was in class. What awesome feelings. I tend to forget about from time to time. The joy I had at this time in my life is something to relive and revisit so I am always present in how and why I am practicing today.

Close your eyes. Take a deep breath and count to ten. Ask yourself this question: When did you make the decision that you wanted to be a registered dietitian?

I am going to throw this out there: becoming and being a Registered Dietitian Nutritionist is friggin hard! Right?!? When I was going through the classes and the internship, there were many times I wondered why in the world I was really doing this. I did not have to change my plans and pursue this new found passion. This is exactly why it is very important to embrace your journey and tell your story. Just like me, you could have chosen a completely different path, but you didn't. When was the last time you took the time to really think of your decision since your whirlwind of undergrad, internship and exam.

Dietetics is a profession that flourishes from personal stories. Dietetics is a field where your journey and your story is very important. I remember each registered dietitian I met and worked with during my internship and I would ask them when did they know they wanted to be a dietitian. This would lead into their very important and personal nutrition story. We all have a story. We all have a connection to this profession, otherwise we would not be here today.

My Journey

After 6 months of what seemed like a very long and grueling internship, my last rotation was my clinical rotation in a trauma hospital. I was given huge opportunities when I was there and experienced more than I could have ever imagined. I was one of the clinical dietitian team members and had the same daily responsibilities as they did. I had a patient list each day, I charted and provided recommendations to physicians and I was there to educate my patients on their nutrition needs. It was exactly what I wanted to do as a registered dietitian. I had the perfect blend of helping others with nutrition and experiencing the environment I would have had as a physician.

During my last month of my internship, I started the job search. In 2001, there weren't the job opportunities like there is now. As a registered dietitian, you were extremely limited to a few major roles, with clinical being one of them. I sent out numerous letters to prospective employers, including clinical, WIC, Extension and Public Health, hoping there would be an opening. Weeks passed, many weeks passed, and I did not hear anything from anyone. Not a peep. I was going to finish my internship and there would be no job. My biggest fear. No grand finale to all my hard work. No opportunity to start my career and my life that I worked so hard to achieve. It sucked and I felt completely defeated. My other friends had started their careers 2 1/2 years ago and now, my life was on hold again. Why did I do this to myself?

When my internship was coming to a close, my preceptors and fellow registered dietitians, Amy, Sherry, Brenda and Kim, thought so highly of me, they offered me my first job. I was ecstatic and felt very lucky to have been given the opportunity. Unfortunately, the job was only part time and around 16 to 20 hours a week. Not the most ideal situation for me, this ambitious registered dietitian crazy person right out of an internship. I was looking for the ideal situation. But not every gift comes in the pretty and perfectly wrapped package.

At the time, I didn't realize what a gift I was given as my first employment opportunity. I was already trained and could jump into all the same responsibilities and privileges of my co-workers. To ease the transition into being an adult and on my own (also known as paying all of my own bills), I luckily had a back-up plan.

In college, when I was on the track to becoming a doctor, I worked at Midwest Dermatology Clinic. During my time there, I gained a lot of experience and discovered another aspect of my passions: pathology and histology. Histology is the study of body tissues, specifically skin. During college, this part-time job helped my books each semester and possibly a few late-night pizzas. I also discovered I was really good at it and enjoyed it. During my internship, they were so wonderful by allowing me to come in during off hours to work to make a little extra gas money. When I did not find anything full time after my internship, the clinic offered me a full-time position to work in their Histology Lab. This could all work! I could work both jobs, have a steady income, health insurance, retirement and all those good things a new ambitious college graduate is looking for.

I had the amazing opportunity to work at both jobs for 7 years. But the jobs and I got a little weary. Working 50 to 60 hours a week became exhausting, and I was realizing I was having difficulty finding the work/life balance I desired. My attitude and well-being started to get very unsteady toward the end. I knew I loved working at the derm clinic and I knew I loved being a clinical dietitian, but I was starting to realize my passion was more for dietetics than it was for skin. I was also realizing my passion in dietetics was using my super nutrition powers to prevent illness and helping people stay in good health.

In the hospital, patients HAVE to see you based on screening criteria and MD consults. The last thing they want to talk about while they are sick and during their stay is what low-sodium foods they can consume after a triple bypass heart surgery. All they want to do is go home and worry about it later. At times, I felt as if I was not making a difference or an impact on the long term wellness of my patients. And then through all this cerebral questioning, I was exhausting myself and becoming a person who was considering not being a registered dietitian anymore.

After feeling that way for almost a year and concluding I needed a change, I started the job hunt again. This process mostly found other clinical jobs that would replicate the same thing I was currently doing with different scenery and lunch offerings in the cafeteria.

My friend Jenny, who I did my internship with, started working for Hy-Vee, a grocery store chain in the Midwest. When she explained what she was doing, the job sounded like something that would fit me and my passions well. Nutrition where it means the most: when you are shopping for the food to fuel your body and feed your family. I got excited of course, but quickly discovered this was not an easy job to come by because it was just hitting the registered dietitian career landscape. After Jenny shared with me the progressive things she was doing at work, I immediately share with her my interest and to let me know if anything became available within the company. I knew I could stay in my jobs until I found something matching my newly discovered goals and purpose as a registered dietitian. I kept hoping and believing I would find it.

And then one day, in the middle of the afternoon while I was working in the lab, I received a call from a Human Resource Department from the same retail grocery store chain Jenny was working for. Kim, the HR manager, asked if I was "interested in applying for a retail dietitian position" in a nearby city. A city I knew nothing about and a grocery store I had never shopped at. Of course, I instantly said yes! No joke. It took me one second blurt out my yes and to jump on this opportunity. I emailed Kim my resume and the next day I was offered an interview for the following week.

For me, this was the unearthing of "it's who you know" in the registered dietitian world when it comes to jobs. We are such a special circle of professionals who support each other from the start of our internships and carries on into employment. We make sincere and lasting connections through different collaborations creating valued respect for each other. I am sure you have had this similar situation happen during your time as an intern or during your career. I still cannot thank Jenny enough for passing on my resume. I never would have guessed, starting out as being in the same internship class with Jenny, beautifully turned into a pretty amazing life-long friendship with a fellow registered dietitian and now a co-worker.

I drove to the unknown city of Des Moines, Iowa, the following week for my interview. Hy-Vee had over 200 stores in the Midwest and the store I would be working in was brand new and opening in 3 months. The job of the retail dietitian was fairly new to the company and was a new position to this particular store. I met with the store director and the Registered Dietitian Supervisor from the corporate office. An hour and a half later, I confidently walked (when really I wanted to run and cheerfully scream) out of the store director's office.

The interview went well. Really well. It felt comfortable from the start, and I had this warm and fuzzy feeling like I feel when I go home. It was very weird to feel this way in an interview. Maybe for my lack of interview experience because I didn't have to with my previous job? Maybe because it was because my passion and purpose were colliding in my future professional home. I walked out feeling confident but fearful I was not even close to what they were looking for in a registered dietitian. Oh, and then, there was the thought of moving, starting a brand new job that had never existed at this location before, basically starting all over again. It scared the shit out of me. It was the longest 2 hour drive of my life.

After I returned home and went over the interview a thousand times in my head, I truly felt I didn't get the job. They probably had plenty of other more qualified candidates, I had never worked in retail in any capacity and I was not from the city. The next day, I went back to work and continued to live in what now felt like my "settled-for" professional life. I continued the job search in Omaha and would endure my current jobs until I felt the same way about a job like I did during my interview at the grocery store.

Two weeks later, my future boss called and offered me the job. WHATTTTT??? REALLY? Not what I was expecting AT ALL! I was shocked and excited for this new and much welcomed adventure. Sure there was the fear of really starting all over, but that feeling had nothing on how I was feeling about my current jobs. I am not going to lie, I did everything I could to talk myself out of it, but my inner being kept telling me this was the right choice. I would leave my comfort zone of a city I knew well, a comfortable home, close friends and family and jobs that were not making me happy or fulfilling my passion and purpose. This was the key phrase influencing me to say yes:

And jobs that were not making me happy or fulfilling my passion and purpose.

> *You spend most of your time working and sleeping.*
> *So you best have a job you love and an amazing bed.*
> - Anne Elizabeth, Registered Dietitian, Author
> and Now What? Expert.

So that's exactly what I did. I accepted the job where I currently work, packed up my things and moved to Des Moines, Iowa, and bought a really amazing, kick-ass comfy bed. There were moments during this major leap in my life, I wished the amazing bed had magical powers to make the transition from a clinical registered dietitian to a retail registered dietitian a little smoother.

I am going to describe clinical dietetics in one word: structured. I will now describe retail dietetics in one word: scattered. In 2008, retail registered dietitians were a new and emerging field. I was more enamored with the idea of the position, more than really knowing what the position involved. I was joining a grocery store chain that had been around for 75 plus years, and was starting a fairly newer position to the entire company.

Not only did I not really know what I was doing, neither did my boss, managers or coworkers. I had some corporate support, guidance and training, but really I had to dig out my registered dietitian compass and navigate this frontier on my own. This was onerous and complete opposite of my previous job which made it actually thrilling.

As a clinical registered dietitian, we have guidelines and criteria for almost everything we do. Each day at work was always well defined and met the controlling needs of crossing off each bullet point on the the beautifully constructed Type A personality checklist of mine. On the flip side, each day of being a retail registered dietitian starts out with great intentions of an orchestrated checklist and usually ends with the question "where did my checklist go and what was I doing again?" The newness was overwhelming and beautifully chaotic at times, but the job has proved to be 100% worth it.

My Passion

Which brings me to present day and 8 years later. I continue to work at one of the best jobs a registered dietitian could have but I know my journey continues. I know if I stop exploring and experiencing what this profession has to offer, then I am not fulfilling the most important part of my life: my passions. This book, this small but mighty piece of my inner workings, is nourishing another branch of my journey....

I have learned to never stop exploring my journey and I have also learned to not to intricately follow my passions. When I was listening to a podcast, Mike Rowe (host of Dirty Jobs) said something resonating deep within me:

Never follow your passion, but always bring it with you.

Being a registered dietitian is an ever-evolving profession and, now more than ever, there are so many stunning opportunities for us. What I once thought was the direction of my passion, isn't so concrete. It's moveable and evolves constantly which is why I will not follow it, but I make sure it is light guiding everything I do. Passion is the fire lighting the way along any journey. This light gives me the flexibility to "go with the flow" in every passionate experience I am in, and it has been working really well for me, I must say. Some of us are very comfortable and happy working in a job for a long time. Some of us have personal situations not allowing us to explore these opportunities. Some of us are like me and need to keep growing and trying new things. Whatever your situation and desires, you are a registered dietitian, and whatever is working is great as long as you're taking care of your needs. You have already conquered school, an internship and your exam which is hardest tangible part of our profession. Now is the time to focus on you, focus on your passions and conquer your next and most important quest: being the greatest and best damn registered dietitian you always wanted and dreamed of being.

If you organize you life around your passion, you can turn your passion into your story and then turn your story into something bigger-something that matters.

- Blake Mycoskie; is an American entrepreneur, author, and philanthropist.

Two

Purpose

*I have come here to chew bubblegum and kick ass,
and I'm all outta bubblegum.*
- George Nada, the main protagonist in
John Carpenter's movie *They Live.*

Purpose. What is my purpose? A tough and extremely loaded question, I know, but very important nonetheless. It is common to believe passion and purpose are one in the same. Nope, sorry, they are two different things. We need to have passion and we need to know what that passion is, but we need purpose to execute our passion. Purpose is the reason you journey.

Have you ever felt a longing for something but you are not sure what it is?

Personally, I have recurring thoughts of wanting something delicious to eat, a craving I can't seem to pinpoint. In the process, I consume an abundance of different foods and calories, and I never really find the exact food that fulfills my craving. Discovering what you crave and finding what brings you melt-in-your-mouth satisfaction is exactly what your purpose and life's mission is.

Why am I on this earth? What do I want to do with this one precious life I have been given? What don't I suck at?

Purpose is not obvious and easy to identify. Purpose presents itself by knowing, living and acting on your passion. You need to be in the midst of it, working with your passion and working toward that purpose to see results. It is important to rethink the questions you are asking yourself to help you with defining your purpose.

What do I want to spend my time and energy on which will fulfill me but also help others?

What am I willing to work on, put effort into, maybe struggle and even accept possible failure?

What makes me forget my favorite TV show is on or makes me forget to eat and drink because the thrill of what I am doing is better than any other thing?

If you are just thinking about it, you will not get very far. As you go through this journey, you will gain wisdom and insight into yourself as a person and as a registered dietitian. You will learn that you need to explore different areas of our awesome profession to get closer to providing you clarity. Once you start exploring, you will start feeling yourself get closer to what brings you joy. You will get out of your head and more in tune with what inspires and motivates your inner truth and your reason you journey. These will be puzzle pieces connecting your sense of purpose. It will evolve and change more than your passion will because you will change and advance in your career. You will experience moments of certainty that you have finally figured out your purpose, only to realize it evolves once again.

Give purpose time, and be gentle with yourself. Not everything needs to be on a to-do list or time schedule. If something is consistently on your mind, do not give up on it. Keep working toward it and don't let it go. Purpose does not need to be extreme or flamboyant, it can be very simple and still be purposeful. With your passion being the root of your life, purpose is the tree of your life with many branches.

When you feel unsatisfied or have the feeling of emptiness, this is the time to fertilize your tree with passion so new branches start to grow your purpose. I want you to radiate your passion of nutrition. I want it to beam from your eyes and your face. I want you to know what being fulfilled from your profession feels like. I want you to purposely keep choosing dietetics as your profession. I want you to feel connected and I want you to feel great every day about the answers you that have materialized in your life through purposeful discovery. How you decide to spend your time is the legacy you will leave on this earth and it has to feel incredible.

Since most of us really do not know our purpose, I think it is important to work through some personal questions to help you identify purpose in your life and most importantly in your career. We have no idea how long we will be on this earth to live our passion and purpose, so it is important to explore these questions to find our true happiness within our profession. Take the time to explore what truly feels important to you as a registered dietitian.

I will ask myself these questions often to recenter myself. Sometimes I get sidetracked or discouraged about my career and these questions either reel me back in or help me determine if I need to change my focus.

1. **What fuels your fire?**

   What gives you that warm and fuzzy feeling when it comes to your job? Or what lights a fire under your ass and gets you fired up and invested? Each of us has internal fires that need to be stoked. If that stoking is not happening in your current job or career, then you are not getting the fuel you need for your passion. Your passion is the fuel that keeps the fire burning for your daily work. You need to keep feeding your flame to stay passionate about being a registered dietitian, so you need to know what keeps your fire going. You need to strike while the iron is hot and is tapping into your emotions. If you find yourself feeling excited, happy, inquisitive, uncomfortable or mad, you are getting closer to unveiling your purpose.

2. **What is it about being a registered dietitian that matters most?**

   Do you find yourself getting into a daily routine and going through the motions of your day? Are you distracted when you are practicing your passion by just doing enough or do you find yourself all-in when you are in your job? What is it that gets you out of bed each day and takes you to your job? If you didn't have to go to your job each day, if it was optional and you would still get paid, would you still go? How you answer these questions will hopefully tell you what matters most. I can honestly say in the first part of my career, I got to the point that I would have not gone to work, even if I still got paid. I would have done a zillion other things. That is when I knew, I was not being a registered dietitian who felt anything I did mattered. This is an example of not living your professional purpose.

3. **What did not work in the past, what is working in the present and what do you want for your future?**

   If a particular job did not work for you in the past, I hope you learned something and you do not try to do it again. Please! It is not like trying a new vegetable a few times. I know there are a lot of factors into working at a job you love (co-workers, location, salary) but what about the actual work? It is ok to admit that maybe this particular job was not the right fit for you as a registered dietitian when you take the other components out of the equation and focus on the work. There is not a one-size-fits-all jon for registered dietitians. What *is* working presently? Find the positive aspects of your career and really understand why they are working to help fulfill you professionally. By knowing what didn't work and knowing what is currently working, will help determine what your bright future should look like. This knowledge enables you to seek out jobs, volunteer opportunities and collaborations that will create a lifetime of purpose. And guess what? They make you feel happy!

4. **Have you failed and do you want to keep going?**

I hope you have attempted many different things in the field of dietetics (or plan on doing so). I hope you have succeeded, but I also hoped you have failed. If you have failed at something and you were content not ever trying it again. Perfect, now you know it was not for you. But if you have failed at something and want to keep trying, well that surely is giving you a pretty clear view of your purpose. You have embraced failure and you are willing to find different angles on making it work. That is profound, scary and lovely all at the same time.

5. **Is what you are doing solving a problem and making a difference?**

Purpose is about internal satisfaction with how you are solving a problem. We are registered dietitians, and there are a bazillion problems in this world when it comes to nutrition. As nutrition experts, we can be an important part of solving those problems. Pick one you are an expert in or feel strongly about. You do not have to think globally (just yet), but locally is a great place to start. We all have our own networks of friends, family, neighborhoods, religious and education communities, and cities. How are you solving a problem within your network, how are you making a difference?

As you read through these questions, make sure to answer them honestly. Do not let yourself get distracted by security. We all feel secure when we are willfully employed. Being employed means nothing, if you are not doing it with purpose.

Find something you're passionate about and keep tremendously interested in it.

- Julia Child, was an American chef, author, and television personality.

Three

Finding Joy

Always serve too much hot fudge sauce on sundaes. It makes people overjoyed and puts them into your debt.
- Judith Olney, is a cookbook author, a cooking school teacher, and a former restaurant critic and food editor at the Washington Times.

I had an acquaintance who always talked about being humble and he was deeply troubled by people who were not. His thoughts and sincere concern made me question being humble myself and if being humble was being on the right path. After defining being humble and what it means in my life, I really   do not feel anyone needs to be humble or needs to humble themselves. When you are humble it means you are lowering yourself or someone else in dignity and importance. What I do think we need to find in our lives is gratitude and joy. I think being grateful is much more profound and significant than being humble.

There are many days I find it difficult to find one good thing happening over the course of the day. The not-so-good things tend to over power and make me forget the all good things. During a difficult year of no-so-great things happening in my life, Amanda, a dear friend of mine and fellow registered dietitian, gave me the most precious gift. It was a large mason jar decorated in my favorite colors of pink, purple and white adorned with a tag labeled: ***Anne's Giant Jug of Happiness***. This jug was meant for me to start giving gratitude to the great things happening in my life by remembering and writing them down each day.

This has completely changed my life and perspective both personally and professionally.

At the end of the work day, I date a small piece of paper and I write down one joy (or if there is more than one, super!, I write them all down!) happening during the day that is registered dietitian and job related. First of all, it is great to end the day by centering myself and revisiting the positives that have occurred. When I leave the office, whatever happened that day, is left at the door. I have found this has made me a happier person and has given me the ability to honor my work/life balance. At the end of each month, I empty my giant jug of joy and read the positives that have happened and center myself on all the greatness gracing my life.

Joys can be simple or they can be more involved. When you are writing them, put down enough detail to recreate the feeling you had when it happened that day. This is an example of one of my work joys: *Today, an adult customer tried Brussels sprouts after telling me he did not like them and it changed his mind. His 5-year-old son watched him eat it and wanted to try them too. They bought a bag for dinner that evening. Big win!*

After reading it, I can still remember this particular day and the dad's face after he tried a vegetable he just knew he didn't like. The best part was the son looking up at his dad and wanting to be just like him. That's when I knew I made a difference. That is when I felt joy down in my heart and it was definitely a joy worth reliving.

This joy jar helps you realize (or maybe don't realize) the happiness you have in your job and if you are in the right place of your journey. It will also will help remind you of why you became a registered dietitian in the first place and continue to feel confident in your purpose. When you read your joys, it will give you a "feeling" about your current employment. The feeling might be "this job is right where I need to be" or it could start giving you signs that maybe it is time for a change. If it is hard to write something down at the end of the day, it is time for a little perspective. You know yourself the best and only you can tell when things are great or when things might need to change. Life gets busy, joys are not celebrated and goals and aspirations can be forgotten.

Celebrating joy is the best way to end the day on a positive note. Being a registered dietitian is not a "leave work at work" kind of job. We become very invested in our clients, customers and co-workers and sometimes it can carry over into our personal lives. Celebrating daily joy boosts your aliveness, gives you confidence and decreases your risk for burnout. When you give your joys recognition, it is the gift that keeps on giving. You are giving yourself the high fives you deserve, the thanks you may not receive, achievement of goals you have set and the ability to take the time to really soak in and reflect on the professional experiences you have.

Do not only celebrate joys at work, but continue celebrating them at home and outside of work. This is where that little thing called "work/life balance" comes into play. When home is in balance, work tends to be in balance. To have this, you need to be in tune with registering gratitude and experiencing daily joy.

Since I have given space in my life to this gratitude and joy ritual, my life feels compellingly happier and healthier. I take the time to reflect in all different aspects of my life, stop focusing on the negative, renew my energies that build my character and make myself a stronger person with my work family and my home family. There is no joy to small or too big to celebrate.

What was your joy today?

Talking about our problems is our greatest addiction.
Break the habit. Talk about your joys.
- Rita Stein ED.D., Educational and Corporate Consulting Bilingual and intercultural Communication specialist.

Now What? Worksheet

Now What? Worksheet

I want you to take time to put YOU at the forefront of your headspace. Clear your mind of everything else that consumes your mind and your day. These "now whats" are for you to help determine your passion and purpose.

Exercise #1: Write Your Story

Find a quiet place to sit, armed with a piece of paper and a pen and reflect back to when your journey started with dietetics. Ask yourself these questions: When did you make the decision that you wanted to be a registered dietitian? Why did you decide this was the profession for you? Take 10 minutes and write down all the thoughts that come to mind when you think about these questions. Think of this as your "elevator speech" when your inquisitive intern asks your story.

Exercise #2: Write Your Purpose

Go to a place that inspires, relaxes you and/or makes you happy. Take 2 to 3 deep breaths, and, on the third breath, close your eyes. Ask yourself how did you become a registered dietitian? Think back to your first job or maybe that is the job you are in right now. What did you feel about your first job? Was it or is it something you love? Do you want to move on? If you moved on, why? Once you explore these thoughts, open your eyes. Write down things that you think about when you think about each job you have had as a registered dietitian. This is your personal journey with your profession. You are shaping your professional life with each job you do as a registered dietitian. And if you do not want to get burned out, you need to keep going back on what works for you and what does not. This will help lead you to the job you love, your purpose, if you haven't already found it.

Exercise 3: Write Your Joys

You are reading this book because you have a need for something, right here and right now, in your life. Find a place that you will walk by or be everyday. Place a jar or any container, a pad of paper and a writing utensil in that spot. At the end of the day, write the date and the joy you experienced that day.

Joy Stage 1: Read your joys every week on Sunday evening for 4 weeks. Keep the significant joys that really stand out to you in a resealable bag.

Joy Stage 2: Read your joys on the last Sunday of the month for weeks 8 and week 12. Add the additional significant joys that really stand out to you to the resealable bag.

Joy Stage 3: Read your joys every 3 months. Keep the significant joys that really stand out to you in a resealable bag. Repeat Stage 3 until you reach 1 full calendar year after you started. At the end of the year, reread the significant joys in your resealable bag.

Joy Stage 4: Smile, laugh, cry and embrace the true joy you have in your life.

Part Two:

Part Two:

So You Landed the Job?

Pleasure in the job puts perfection in the work.

Four

Your Nutrition Philosophy

It is more fun to talk with someone who doesn't use long, difficult words but rather short, easy words like "What about Lunch?
- A. A. Milne, was an English author, best known for his books about the teddy bear Winnie-the-Pooh and for various poems.

A few years ago, a prospective client called my office and asked a lot of professional questions about me and my practice. He wanted to know where

I went to school, if I liked to cook and if I exercised. Then he asked "What is your nutrition philosophy?"

Insert panic mode. I had never been asked these types of questions before and then he asks this very loaded question? It was something I had never given much thought to, let alone have an elevator speech prepared to deliver upon demand. "What is my nutrition philosophy?" I have been a dietitian for over a decade and could barely stammer out an answer worthy of this prospective client.

I now understand why this client wanted to know. He wanted to know if I would be a good fit for his wellness journey. If my philosophy did not align with his wellness goals, he already knew it would not be a successful relationship. Kudos to him for being such an advocate for his health and his goals. He knew what he wanted and needed for his success.

It was my "a-ha" moment. I know I am passionate about being a registered dietitian, but what I really needed to do was sit down and figure out my nutrition philosophy. By having this tool, I would be better prepared to connect with the right clients, set the right professional goals for myself to keep learning and growing my brand and to properly carry out the work I am so passionate about.

If this is something you have not done either, I highly recommend this being the first and most important step a registered dietitian complete and have ready before you start your first job. I was completely late to the game by not knowing my answers and not giving him the answers he wanted to hear. If you are like me, it is not too late! You will get asked this question by someone, and hopefully, you will continue to ask yourself this question during your career.

I feel as registered dietitians, we can help everyone and anyone with their nutritional needs, but can we help them well and meet them where they are at in their wellness journey? Your philosophy is the fundamental nature of how you practice as a registered dietitian. It is your core values, beliefs, ideas, tenets and school of thought. Once you know this, it makes it easier to be the registered dietitian you want to be and believe in. It does not mean you need to be an expert in everything to meet everyone's nutritional needs.

I quickly realized this is not an easy task and it took me much contemplation, scribbles and wadded-up papers on my living room floor to compile my own. How could something I practiced every day be so difficult to formulate into sentences? Because I struggled with preparing my own philosophy, at the end of this section, I have provided you a worksheet to get your juices flowing and provide some direction in your own personal development. I am bravely sharing my own as an example of how I have formulated mine. To get me started, I thought of my philosophy as a recipe, carefully constructed to provide the most flavorful and well-constructed product.

Anne's "Core Value" Stir Fry

Ingredients:

1 cup Science

1 cup Food

1 cup Portion Sizes

1 cup Meditation

1 cup Sleep

1 cup Physical Activity

1 cup Joy

Instructions:

1. Nutrition information is based on science and should be distributed by a Registered Dietitian.

2. It's Your Wellness Journey. I will meet you exactly where you are.

3. "One size does not fit all" when it comes to living the healthiest life you are capable and willing to live.

4. There is no "bad-for-you food," there are just "bad-for-you portion sizes."

5. Food first, always.

6. Life is too short. Take time to fuel your life (cooking and eating), take time to breath (meditate), take time to rest (sleep, 7 to 8 hours), and take time to move (physical activity). The rest of the day, take time to be gracious, kind, to love and be loved.

7. Find the joy in everyday.

There is nothing glamorous or profound about my philosophy or principles, but it is something I practice with myself and would practice with my family and friends. I share this with potential clients before we even start working together because I want them to be successful and to receive the most beneficial wellness guidance from a professional. Maybe I am not the right registered dietitian for them?

Mostly importantly, I do not want to waste their time or waste my own. By producing and establishing my professional philosophy, I am completely comfortable telling them I am not an expert in everything but I know or will find a registered dietitian who is. If I cannot assist them with their wellness journey, I make it a point to know a great network of nutrition professionals to refer them to.

I am very thankful to this man who asked me this very important question that day. With his inquisitiveness, I realized how important it is to establish the foundation of my philosophy. When you have this core foundation to work with, you establish the registered dietitian you truthfully are. Yes, things will change as your and our profession changes. Once you have written it, it does not mean it is a final draft. By keeping your foundation in place, you can always change and adapt the principles supporting your philosophy.

At the end of this section is a worksheet I started developing the the evening after I had the conversation with my prospective client. After that mind-blowing phone call, I realized how important my philosophy is and I knew it would be just as important for someone else in the future. I have created this to help you work with your philosophy. Please take the time to really think about it and give yourself enough time to make it an all-encompassing working document for you. Connect with other dietitians if it helps to get new ideas and thoughts. It will not happen in an afternoon or a day and it may take you a little while to work through it. Once you have established your framework, write it out, type it into a document you can save and change as needed. Keep it simple, one sentence or bullets are just fine, but make it memorable, something you will not forget and something you will come back to when you are questioned or when you question yourself.

Another key is you need to live it each day. As you live it each day, you make the choice to be the registered dietitian you believe you are by following your own tenets. This keeps you consistent and credible and the best testimonial you can give someone. Sharing "I live this philosophy everyday at home and at work" makes it personal and relatable to potential clients and customers. Your philosophy will help you feel good and confident about your professional life. It also gives meaning to what you are doing and why you are doing it. Keep this available for yourself to read and remind yourself who you are as a registered dietitian. It is a useful tool in writing your own biography if you are ever asked to present for a group or organization. The best thing about this written piece of work, your work, is that it comes from a very honest and personal place.

I am slow to learn and slow to forget that of which I have learned. My mind is like a piece of steel-very hard to scratch anything on it, and almost impossible after you get it there to rub it out.
- Abraham Lincoln, the 16th President of the United States.

(Understanding) Your Competition

Women belong in the kitchen. Men belong in the kitchen.
Everyone belongs in the kitchen. The kitchen has food.
- Unknown

Y ou have heard throughout your undergrad and internship the importance of being a registered dietitian. We are THE nutrition experts. First of all, we know the blood, sweat and tears we put into being registered dietitians. We put in long hours, spend lots of money, complete many papers and projects, volunteer, and take ANY nutrition-related job experience just to pad our resumes. If you haven't heard or realized by now, this registered dietitian thing is no joke. So how in the world does a person that takes a 12-hour online course to become a 'nutritionist" become your competition?

Not only are the nutritionists of the world your competition, but any health "guru" becomes your competition, along with a laundry list of others. This list includes anyone who writes about food, anyone who prepares and cooks food, anyone who has eaten food, anyone who has had a weight loss journey or has overcome a food intolerance, anyone who works at a gym, anyone who sells supplements for a company, anyone who has an interest or works in health. These people are anyone and they are everywhere.

What you need to remember is what makes you different from the rest of these individuals and make it known. You know the science and you support your nutrition knowledge based on science- or evidence-based practices. You know how the body works (remember the joys of anatomy and physiology, biochemistry, and microbiology) based on the classes you took in college and then you applied this knowledge during your rotations of your internship.

There is a reason why you took those classes because everything comes together when you practice. You know what your body does chemically and physically when it ingests a carbohydrate, and to further this knowledge, you know what happens when an individual with celiac disease consumes a carbohydrate food containing wheat. It is not a simple "it makes my stomach hurt," it is much more.

Anyone with a health interest and touts it as their profession started out the same way you did - with a story, journey and now a philosophy. People relate with these individuals, and this is why they gain momentum as experts because of a personal connection. People are looking for someone, anyone, who has a personal experience similar to theirs and then they cling to him or her. The connection is greater than the degree or credentials for many people. This is why we need to keep reminding ourselves and the public what sets us apart.

Sometimes as registered dietitians, we get caught up in our expertise. We forget our clients are human and need a human side when we are educating them. We are full of scientific information, but if we cannot make this information relatable to our clients, they will find another "expert" who will. We also have to remember everything starts and ends with food. We became registered dietitians because we wanted to practice preventative health with food. Everyone eats and always will. If we remember this as the foundation and connection with our clients, we will prevail as the nutrition expert.

Have you ever done an internet search for nutrition? What pops up? Registered dietitian does not come up in the first page of most internet searches. Many reputable sources do appear, but our actual profession and title does not come up. Our profession continues to struggle in breaking out in the nutrition world. I struggle with this myself. It drives me crazy! I struggle because the registered dietitian should be the first thing that comes up in a nutrition search. This is exactly why we need to understand our competition. Where do our clients, who so desperately need our help, really go to get their nutrition information?

Our profession, meaning YOUR profession, needs you to be the biggest advocate. We need to toot our own horns and I know this is not easy for many of us. No one else is going to tout or advertise your expertise, if you do not. If you are passionate about your profession, you need to be proactive and be the face of nutrition in your community and on all media avenues.

It is important to know where individuals seek nutrition information. The internet is the single-handed most popular place to seek out this information. Health-related searches are in the top 3 of all searches on the internet. This is why more and more people tend to trust bloggers and other health gurus.

Here is a great example:

In a national survey of more than 1,000 moms done in 2013 by Flieshman-Hillard and TheMotherhood.com, 96% of American mothers were planning on making changes to their food buying habits based on what is driving moms' consumer behaviors in meal planning, grocery shopping and meal preparation as well as what is influencing their food purchasing decisions, such as bloggers and online peers as a trusted source over dietitians and doctors.

Here it is in plain writing and one encompassing word: **Heartbreaking**

We must understand the needs of our audience. I believe people are thinking about food more and more throughout the day by searching for recipes and nutrition information on food-based web sources or social media sources. I know this because I do the same thing myself for my own personal interest. It is 3 pm, and I have no idea what I am going to make for dinner, so I grab my trusty smartphone, tap on my Pinterest app and see what I can find. If I am doing this, think of how many other individuals are doing the same thing.

In 2015, The International Food Information Council Foundation conducted their Food and Health Survey: *Consumer Attitudes toward Food Safety, Nutrition and Health* by surveying over 1,000 Americans ages 18 to 80. It is weighted to represent the demographics of the United States. Last year, in 2015, almost half of all Americans surveyed have given a lot of thought to the healthfulness of foods and beverages they consume.

Here are some other interesting findings of the survey:

- Consistent with previous years, more than half of Americans rate their own health as excellent or very good and this group is actually overweight or obese based on BMI data collected.

- Four out of five Americans are trying to lose weight or maintain their current weight.
- When they were asked which of the following they have used in your efforts to import the healthfulness of their diet, these were the result
  - Family and Friends: 32%
  - Weight Loss Plan: 22%
  - App to track food: 22%
  - Medical professional: 22%
  - Registered Dietitian: 6%
  - Blog, support group, online community: 6%
- Personal Healthcare Professionals are most trusted for information on both types of food and food safety.
  - Health Professionals (including doctors, nurses, physician assistants, nurse practitioners and registered dietitians) 65%
  - Friend or family member: 29%
  - US Government Agencies: 42%
  - Food Expert on television: 24%
  - Health food and nutrition bloggers: 24%

Based on this study, there is an obvious need for registered dietitians to assist those trying to live a healthier lifestyle and to lose or maintain their weight. But when individuals are seeking out help, family, friends, weight loss plans, apps and OTHER medical professionals are winning, while registered dietitians are losing. 6% of individuals seek out a registered dietitian in this survey and that search is tied to blogs, support groups and online communities. We know they are not the nutrition experts, but the public is not getting the message.

Look at the community in which you practice, who is your competition? Are there people within a 30 miles radius of where you work that potential clients are going to for nutrition information instead of you?

An easy way to determine who is the competition around you is by doing an internet search (make sure to include Facebook, Pinterest, Twitter, Instagram, Vine, Healthy Aperture) of topics such as nutrition, weight loss, food allergies, sports nutrition, cooking, eating healthy, food bloggers and supplements. When you see what is happening around you, you devise a plan to keep you as the leader of the pack. Get to know them, read what they are writing and talking about, who they are talking to and with, know their credentials and backgrounds. Discover how they relate with their customer base and tap into their audience by reading comments and dialogues from readers. Chances are, if they are in your community, you know someone personally who has some type of connection to them. These people can be the conduit in helping you understand your competition.

Here is are the common (but not inclusive) list of people you want to know in your community:

- Medical Professionals (Doctors, Nurses, Physician Assistants, Nurse Practitioners)
- Chiropractors
- Wellness Coordinators
- Bloggers
- Twitter
- Distributors for supplement companies
- Nutrition Stores/Salespersons
- "Foodies"
- Chefs
- Fitness Programs and Instructors
- Nutritionists
- Dietitians (not registered)
- Health Coaches
- Health Educators
- Athletes
- Gyms and Athletic Trainers
- Self-Proclaimed "Nutrition Experts"
- Wellness Spas
- Fitness and Wellness Infomercials
- Contract Management Companies
- Dietary Managers

- Food Service Managers
- Insurance Companies

All these people have some sort of nutrition connection. Many of them do it because of some kind of experience they have had or it is something they are interested in.   Take a second to think about social interactions in a workplace. If someone has had a wellness breakthrough, such as losing weight, other people want to know exactly how they did it. When the person tells them how, it becomes education and a plan others can follow verbatim, devising the "It worked for her, it will work for me" plan.

Another component of the survey I mentioned above was "Over one-third or 35% of those surveyed used no one to aid in the healthfulness of their diet." If we added this percentage to the measly 6% we received, we would be on the forefront for nutrition information of individuals surveyed.

There are many weight loss programs and fitness programs that succeed, become popular and make a lot of money by passing along this information. There is no scientific background, but there are tangible and visible results of those participating in a program that is easily passed on by word of mouth. This happens for registered dietitians as well, but we are not the quick fix so many people are seeking. We don't provide the "magic bullet" people are mesmerized by. What we do have is the knowledge to provide sound and lifelong information that is not a temporary solution, resulting in the long term results individuals are truly seeking.

When you start to compete and use your greatest assets as the nutrition expert, you can too, penetrate this inner circle of those seeking out wellness. We need to be right there, where the need is and we need to be providing the solutions. We can easily be the ones developing healthy lifestyle plans, creating recipes with beautiful pictures, starting your own online support community and putting it out there against our competitors. Why the hell not? Why not us?

How do you get started?

There are many ways you can stay ahead of the nutrition curve and that means getting active inside and outside of your job. Of course, we all love the idea of going to work at 8 am and leaving at 5 pm, going home and not giving work a second thought. But again, if being a nutrition expert is your passion, it should continue every day, all day. It does not need to overtake your life, but remember your philosophy? You need to be living it!

Eight years ago, I WAS the registered dietitian who went to work and forgot it when I went home. Because I was in a job I became less passionate about, I did not want to think about nutrition at all when I wasn't there. In return, I was the one who suffered and became the most unhealthy me by not living out my philosophy. I stopped eating well, sleeping well and did minimal physical activity. My billboard for nutrition (my body and attitude) was torn and tattered, appeared unhealthy and looked like hell.

I decided two significant things at that point: I needed to change my job and I needed to repair my nutrition image. But not only when it was required of me and when I was working, but ALL the TIME. This is another area where our competition is kicking us in the ass. They are practicing their passion ALL THE TIME. They incorporate it into their daily lives, at work, at play, at social events with friends or peers, in writing, in photos, in reading, in mindfulness and in rest.

As I transitioned into a new professional role, the passion rejuvenated itself and I refurbished my obviously tattered billboard into a new and improved one. Working and living my passion all day long was easy to do with a fresh professional start. It might not be easy for those of us that cannot change that part of our life but always remember, even a few changes can rejuvenate you and place you right there in the race with our competitors.

1. Keep current on trending topics.

Your competition stays abreast of all things health and wellness. They stay in tune with hot topics and find an interest in them. We need to do this as well. Once someone knows you are a registered dietitian, they will ask you questions about an article they read on Facebook or what supplement was recommended on their favorite daytime television show. Know what is happening and what your response will be. This is the easiest way to compete in simple everyday conversation with those you encounter on a daily basis.

2. Be social.

Be present on social media, take photos and make videos. Start talking about current topics of interest on your social media sites. If you see an article on Facebook, chime in and let them know you are a registered dietitian and what your thoughts are. Share an article or topic of interest and open it up for questions from the public. Create conversation surrounding sound nutrition information. Ask your network what they think or if they have any questions you can answer as the nutrition expert. Share the love and support other registered dietitians who are active in the social media landscape. This is very important! By reading, listening commenting, and sharing their content, you show support and confidence in their expertise. You also create a network of other experts to tap into for knowledge and experience when you need it.

I recommend sharing personal stories if you have had an experience with a nutrition- or health-related topic that is trending. For example, I recently shared how I found a new way to make one of my grandma's famous cookie recipes a little healthier. I invited a group of friends over to try it, made a 30-second video of what they thought and included pictures of my friends, the mouthwatering cookies and the recipe.

By starting a conversation on a regular basis, your network will talk with you, and, in return, they will encourage their network to talk with you too. Take photos and make mini videos of things you do that you are passionate about. Whether it is a picture of the beautiful and healthful dinner you just prepared or an interview of a success story of someone you worked with and helped with their health. All you need is your smartphone, no fancy equipment necessary.

Your friends and family will think it is really cool they know a registered dietitian. They will share this in conversations they have with others. "My friend Anne is a registered dietitian and she said this…." or have you seen Anne's blog, check out this post she shared the other day. This gives me a happy heart and is very rewarding that others are listening and are interested in my expertise. Your friends and family are your biggest advocates and can help you with your competition.

3. Start a blog, video blog (vlog) or audio blog (podcasting).

My initial venture into writing was starting a blog, Nutritional Noshes. At the time, it became another outlet of my personal interest of writing. It did not start out as nutrition all day every day, but it became the journal of Anne, a registered dietitian, and Anne, a human being with family, friends, parties, adventures, and personal experiences. Some days, I post about nutrition; some days, I post about something or someone I love. I put my favorite quotes in there and I talk about different aspects of my life. This gives me a personal and human connection to the public and to my clients. It makes me more like the competition listed above and not only establishes me as a professional in the social media world but also as a person. I sure do eat pizza, I love music and inspirational quotes. I do things outside of my job that make me just like my neighbor. I tell stories about myself, so people find a connection with me and want to know me. If they find a connection, they will most likely seek me out for nutrition advice when they need it.

Each week, I receive emails and comments from clients and customers. I also meet new friends, clients and customers who graciously read my blog. If this is something that interests you and you want to get started, there is a great article and advice from registered dietitian Toby Amidor called "Calling All Food Bloggers."

While at FNCE in 2015, I attended the session "Claim the Spotlight! Beyond Traditional Media: Videos, Podcasting, and Self Publishing" presented by Registered Dietitians Melissa Joy Dobbins and Julie Beyer. I had just started listening to podcasts on my commute to work and found this concept fascinating for registered dietitian. This presentation inspired me to consider highlighting my expertise, passions and personal interests through podcasting and as a compliment to my blog. It is another way our competition is succeeding and now is the perfect time for registered dietitians to establish a strong presence over the airwaves.

4. Seek out others that are like minded.

There are many groups of people living where you live, who have similar interests as you, who are not your family or friends. It could be other professionals, non-profit interest groups, businesses, churches, small groups or the person you see walking each morning in your neighborhood. And just as a friendly reminder, it is up to you to start a conversation. One morning, I was out in my yard getting ready to mow the lawn and someone who lives 2 streets over from me, came over to say hi. As we started talking, he asked what I did. When I told him I was a registered dietitian, he was so excited. He had a small men's group that met once a month and asked if I would be interested to come talk with their group about basic nutrition and to answer questions the members might have. What an amazing connection that started in the front of my house!

I spoke to the group of men, who fired a ton of nutrition questions, which I was not expecting. One of the men in the group worked for a company that was looking at doing some wellness initiatives in their office and he asked if it was something I was interested in doing. Of course! In any situation, you never know what could come out of it and no opportunity is too small or insignificant. I met 15 men who were professionals in my community who now all have a connection to me. This single opportunity has brought me into other aspects of their lives and I have become "their dietitian."

5. Cook.

Ok, I will be honest, I am far from a gourmet cook, but over the years being in the retail dietitian role and working closely with my favorite chef in the world, Chef Stacey, I have become a better cook and more relatable to people who struggle with the same thing. This may not sound much like an action plan, but food is the basis for everything we do as registered dietitians and food is the basis for everything others do in everyday life.

You need to understand food, how to prepare it, how to make it healthy and taste good and how to share it. Food can be your introduction and your platform to establish you as the nutrition expert. As registered dietitians, we can be pretty inventive when it comes to food and we need to share it with the world. As nutrition experts, we know what we need to eat to live where I would say 90% of our society lives to eat.

You can speak to people through food and if you are a registered dietitian who cooks, you speak loudly. Every time you go to a get-together or party, have dinner with friends, celebrate someone's milestone like a birthday, marriage, baby, new job or retirement, speak to them with food. And no, I do not mean taking fresh veggies and a low-calorie dip, but really speaking to them with food. If you create something beautiful to look at, delicious to eat and healthy, no one will forget it and they will associate the yummy food with you, "their dietitian."

When I went to the men's group to talk, I brought food. When I go on TV and do a segment with a local newscast, I feed the crew afterwards. It is true, a way to a person's heart is through their stomach. When I experiment with a new recipe that is delicious and successful, I take a ton of pictures and I share it with my social network. Think of foods you love, those decadent, indulgent foods and recreate them for giving to others. If you take an indulgent recipe and change ingredients to make it healthier, it does not guarantee the recipe will work. There is science behind recipes and how they perform with certain ingredients.

This is when I consult with my expert, Chef Stacey, to guide me in recipe development. I am an expert in nutrition but not in food science. Proper food science = desirable results and taste. With Chef Stacey's assistance, no one can resist my key lime pie dip or my quick and healthy chicken Parmesan recipe. When you leave their palates and plates wanting more, you create a loyalty between you and them as the nutrition expert who can also cook.

The five action steps above are being used by your competition. They are winning people over by these five simple things. We have time in our lives to start incorporating at least one. Check with your employer as well about possibly making one of these as part of your job description. Not only will you bring awareness of you as the nutrition expert, but you will also bring your employer into the limelight as well.

If you have an important point to make, don't try to be subtle or clever. Use a pile driver. Hit the point once. Then come back and hit it again. Then hit it a third time.
- Sir Winston Churchill, British Statesman, Prime Minister, Author, Nobel Prize Winner.

The Registered Dietitian "Judgement"

One cannot think well, love well, sleep well, if one has not dined well.
-Virginia Woolf, English writer and one of the foremost
modernists of the twentieth century.

Before you ever start or started working as registered dietitian, did you ever feel judged by your peers, friends, family when it came to food? When you worked as a registered dietitian, do you remember being judged for being the nutrition expert who only eats fruits and vegetables?

Along with your competition in the previous chapter, you will experience judgement coming at you from everywhere. Actually, this is a great thing! Seriously. What do I mean by judgement, and how is this great? You are a registered dietitian, a person who is focused on helping others where they are in their wellness journey by eating healthier and how to live a healthier lifestyle.

If being a registered dietitian is your job, there is no way you would eat lasagna, ice cream or have cocktails, right?

When you are recognized as the nutrition professional, people will want to watch what you eat, what groceries you buy, where you dine out and if you exercise. A multitude of registered dietitians, like myself, are opening the doors of their "true life" and welcoming people into their homes by posting pictures of their refrigerators and healthy/not-so-healthy meals they are consuming. Registered dietitians are striving to be known as real people too. The first time you are judged and rejected, it is hard, because you really do not expect it. When you work in a field where helping people is our primary goal, it is heartbreaking when someone does not believe you can help them because of your own personal choices. For every one person who does not value working with you, there is a dozen of others who will.

Unfortunately, in our profession, we are constantly judged and it is important to create some tough skin. I am a retail dietitian and I shop for my groceries at the store where I work. Since I am well known where I work by employees and the community, there is not a shopping trip that goes by where someone doesn't glance in my cart to see what I am purchasing. Of course, there is always someone who will comment on what they see. I completely welcome this. I have nothing to hide and want to show everyone that yes, I do like to eat healthy, but I also enjoy a vast variety of other foods (also known as ice cream bars, pizza and tacos), in moderation. It is good for me to do this so those who work with me, follow me on social media, read my blog and listen to my podcast, know I am human and I love food.

Where I work, we have a lunchroom where all employees eat. It is very apparent that when I join them to dine, almost everyone kind of slides their plates out of my sight because they fear I will say something about what they are eating. I do not judge anyone in the lunchroom because I want those around me to feel comfortable consuming whatever food their hearts and tummies desire. I will occasionally bring my own lunch of pizza and cookies and eat it in front of my coworkers. This does not prevent judgement of myself, but helps humanize me in this situation and teaches me to not judge others with my registered dietitian eye.

You will be judged when it comes to the food you purchase and eat. You will be judged by other peers, other health professionals and just people in general because our profession revolves around food. Food is a very personal thing for people. Here is a perfectly personal example.

I remember when I was younger, I think around 9 years old, my best friend told me he loved carrot cake. I did not like carrot cake and told him it was gross. He was so mad at me because I, his best friend, did not like the same kind of cake he did. He also told me I would not be invited to his birthday party because I did not like it. This scenario was very personal for him and he was so upset.

This is why, as registered dietitians, we do need to take judgement but we cannot dish it out. We must humanize ourselves, let the public see us eat and be aware of what feedback we are going to get in return. I am always prepared for someone to look in my grocery cart and comment on the cereal I buy and the frozen ice cream treats I love. It is totally fine with me.

In a situation like this, I can talk about food with someone. This is why I like this cereal. This is why I like these frozen ice cream treats. Honestly, this is exactly what they are looking for. They want to know why I choose these items. When I can explain my reasoning as a registered dietitian and as a human who also likes to eat, I make the ever so important connection with this person. Sometime later, I may see them again and because of the conversation, it has a created a trust and comfort with them. They might even have the same items in their grocery cart.

Another example I want to share with you is a client who was "shopping" for a registered dietitian to help her with her weight loss goals. She wanted to meet with me in person to see if we would be a fit and this situation welcomed me sharing my nutrition philosophy. When she came into my office, she took one look at me, smiled and said "thank goodness!" I was a little caught off guard because I just met her and we had not yet began discussing anything. She sat down and explained to me how she just did not feel comfortable working with a very thin registered dietitian. How would a thin registered dietitian know what a "fat" person (her words) is going through when they are trying to lose weight? Now, I could have definitely taken this the wrong way, but I knew exactly what she meant. It made me happy she could feel comfortable working with me because she was not intimidated by the weight of the person she was working with. This is judgement at its finest. She was judging the other "thin" registered dietitians strictly on their appearance for supposedly "not knowing" what is was like to struggle with their weight. She ended up feeling very comfortable and we ended up having a great working relationship, with realistic expectations and she met all of her weight loss goals.

There will be times of judgement when nothing you say is right. I remember working with a client who was struggling with her weight, had an answer for every question we talked about and asked me what I would do in each of those situations. I would share my honest opinion, and she would negatively respond with irritation and disbelief. I specifically remember us discussing her sweet tooth and I was offering suggestions of how to work through the cravings and offering healthier options. Her response was simple: "There is no way a dietitian could understand what it is like to have a sweet tooth as bad as mine because I know you eat only healthy foods and never eat anything sweet." Judgement. She had no clue I have a raging sweet tooth and I can honestly say I have eaten three Dove ice cream bars over a course of a day. That is exactly what I did. I shared my Dove ice cream bar story, and when I did, we found our connection. I did understand, I could relate and by showing her a personal side, she let down her guard and realized her goals were stronger than her excuses.

I just want you to be prepared. You will be judged. You will be judged by clients and you will be judged by other registered dietitians. You will be judged on the food you eat, the way you educate, your thoughts on sugar, how often you exercise and how many servings of vegetables you do or don't eat in a day. You will be judged on your stance on nutrition-related topics in something you have said or written. You're catching my drift, right? You will not always have the right answer to fit everyone's needs. You will not always be the perfect registered dietitian or what our public views as the perfect registered dietitian.

However, the best thing you can do is be consistent in your message. Never be wishy washy with your answers, stick to what you believe to be true and follow your philosophy, creating the ever important credibility professionals should establish. There will be people you will not be able to work with because your information does not align or maybe they just don't believe you have eaten three ice cream treats in one day. It took me many years to realize this and that it is ok. I have had a few people walk out of my office and want a refund, never calling me back to set up a follow-up appointment, or calling me again for an interview for an article in a magazine. If the shoe fits, wear it. If it doesn't fit, there is a shoe that will.

When we have become completely free from the need to judge we will also become completely free from the fear of being judged.
- Henri Nouwen, a Dutch Catholic priest, professor, writer and theologian.

Seven

Stuck in a Rut

I spend a lot of time holding the refrigerator door open looking for answers.
- Anonymous

I cannot tell you how many times during my 15 years as a registered dietitian did I feel like I was going insane. I think partly because I am a person who likes to make things happen. I get held up by the way things are always done because it doesn't mean they are always done correctly. I have found in our profession that sometimes there is a mindset of "don't fix what isn't broken." This does not sit well with me, at all, on any day of the week.

I have embraced that nutrition is an ever-evolving, constantly in motion subject and profession. There are some registered dietitians who are willing to evolve with the subject but find it hard to evolve themselves and their practice as the expert. I think our profession is getting younger, more innovative and our opportunities for employment are beyond exciting. Thinking back to your internship, there were generally three core rotations: Clinical, Community and Food Service. Not everyone wants to work as a registered dietitian in these three areas. Most of us, including and especially myself, are looking for more non-traditional roles as registered dietitian.

For the first seven years as a registered dietitian, I was overjoyed to be working as a clinical dietitian in a trauma hospital. I was drawn to the medical side of nutrition because of my initial collegiate desire to be a physician. The variety of the job was exciting to me and it was a great experience to be exposed to a variety of medical nutrition therapy situations.

All of this experience was great and irreplaceable, but after a few years, I started to feel stuck. Then a few more years went by and I started to feel stifled. Two words: mental collapse. I started to have many days where I did not want to go to work and that is when I knew I didn't want to be a registered dietitian who got comfy and compromised career happiness for a paycheck. I didn't want to be someone who stayed at a job for decades because the routine was easy.

I saw my job as a the definition of insanity. Everyday I came to work, I did the same thing and saw a lot of the same patients. I would try to work with doctors to try different ways to help my patients, but the doctors would not consider my recommendations. I provided impeccable nutrition assessments on patients that no one would read. I was frustrated and felt defeated almost every day. I was stuck in a rut and I needed a life-altering change.

You will feel this way at any job you do for a considerable amount of time. Maybe you can weather the rut and maybe your situation requires you to, but you do not have to stick it out because it is comfortable. I thought I had to stick it out because I was comfortable and I really did not know what else was out there for me to do.

There were many positives. I really liked the other registered dietitians I worked with, I knew my role, I knew almost every diagnosis and nutrition intervention that would come my way. I did not take my job home with me. I was financially stable and satisfied. All pretty damn good things when it comes to a job.

But I was not fulfilled and it was only good, not great. I was not living out my passion as a registered dietitian and was going through the daily motions of my job and at times, my own life. I was longing for something different and felt in my core I wanted and needed something more. I wanted to feel like I was making a difference and I was not really getting that from my current situation. I tried to mix things up and bring different ideas to the table, but this was not the job that would allow that. We always have done it this way, so that is the way it is going to be done. I understood at this point, I was the only one who could make the change I was seeking. I was the only one who was going to get myself out of my rut and knew there was so much more waiting for me.

When you find yourself getting stuck, only you can make the change. It might not have to be as drastic as finding a new job. It could be simply educating yourself further, finding and creating the innovation at your current job or taking on a different role as a volunteer requiring your expertise.

Remember when I said nutrition is an ever evolving subject and profession? It is. It is always changing. New information, new studies, new ways of practicing are all out there. It is your responsibility to evolve yourself in any situation you are in or if you are feeling a sincere need for change in your life.

One thing I wish I would have done was taken a gap year in between graduating college and starting my internship. It would have given me time to explore the real world of our profession. Our internships should be a time when we get exposure to all things dietetics. Since most of our internships are very focused on the big picture or they are very specialized, most of us do not get the opportunity to question the assumptions of what we should be doing to integrate real world registered dietitian experiences into our lives.

If you feel you did not get a well-rounded experience during your internship, then why not do it now? To prevent the rut from becoming bigger and deeper, maybe now is the time to create new dietetic "internship-like" exposure to our profession? You are never too old or young to hit the reset button.

When I was in clinical nutrition rotation during my internship, I learned how to do things a certain way from my preceptors that was taught very differently in school. This confirmed there are many different ways to accomplish similar results. By educating or re-educating yourself with a new class or following a mentor in a different working location, it can bring new ideas or ways of doing things to the table. If you are working in an environment where people will listen and be open to new things, the opportunity is there for you to seize it.

If you current situation will not allow you to make changes or you truthfully cannot change jobs, this is where you need to create outlets outside of your job. I looked outside of my employment and really asked myself what other types of things I enjoy doing and how I could marry those with being a registered dietitian. This is why I started writing, cooking more adventurously and sharing pictures/videos of my interests on social media. I do not do it for money or recognition, but I do it because it fulfills me on another level. I reach out to new people, have different conversations and still share my expertise. I have given new life to my passion and have created a network of others who keep my fires burning.

Where are you right now in your profession? Are you in a rut? Have you been in a rut or have had a sense of feeling like you are stuck? It is time to stop going through the motions if you are unsure if you are present in the motions you are part of or creating. We have almost every tool available to us right at our fingertips to access any amount of information we are seeking or anything we are questioning. We need to keep seeking what we need, deep down to our core, to carry our passion with us at all times. This spark within us is not the end all be all compass in our professional lives. What brings you true joy and fulfills you will always link to your passion in someway. You don't have to practice in the guidelines set forth in your internship. You can practice dietetics in many different ways.

Just by preparing a healthy meal full of love for your family or volunteering at a local food bank is practicing dietetics. What sparks your curiosity as a registered dietitian? Always remember, you GET to choose everything in your life: the food you eat, the books you read, the clothes you wear and the soap you use. Think of how much time and energy you put into making those decisions?!? I know you care about your life and the outcomes of your choices, so do not waste time being idle and stuck in an unfulfilling rut.

You are not stuck where you are unless you decide to be.
- Wayne W. Dyer, American philosopher, self-help author, and a motivational speaker.

Eight

Saying Yes and Saying No

Happy has five letters and pizza has five letters. This is not a coincidence.
- Unknown

In my younger years as a registered dietitian, I found myself saying yes to everything. I did not want to pass up on any opportunity, even if I was not sure if I could even do the task. I quickly found what was being asked of me were things no one else wanted to do or did not want to take the time to do it.

I think we can all relate by being the newbie on the block. As new registered dietitians, we are so excited about our profession. Because we are ambitions and full of life, nothing seems too far out of reach. So we say yes and continue to say yes, time after time. And after saying yes to almost everything coming our way, we quickly realize we are in over our heads. I feel by nature, registered dietitians are self-created caretakers. We want to do everything and anything to help people: our clients, our co-workers, our family and our friends. As fresh registered dietitians, we also take on challenges we are unsure about. In our internships, saying no was not an option. But as an employed registered dietitian, you do not have to say yes to everything.

If you are not a new registered dietitian, you may also find yourself saying yes to many things you may not really want to say yes to. Maybe it is another committee, a presentation to write and give, helping a colleague with a task they were asked to do, writing another article or carving out time for a phone interview. There will always be things asked of you because others will always test your willingness to take on more than maybe you can handle. The more you do, the more things are put on your plate or asked of you. It may be a vicious cycle in your work life and even start seeing it invade your personal life.

There are three major ways registered dietitians will be faced with making decisions in saying yes and no:

1. Not everything nutrition will be a fit for you.
For example: I know about diabetes. I can provide basic nutrition education for someone with diabetes, but I am by no means an expert. Early in my practice, I thought I could take on a newly diagnosed individual with diabetes and provide them with the care they needed. And if I didn't know something I would find out along the way. More questions were asked by the patient, therefore resulting in answers I could not provide because I <u>was</u> <u>not</u> the expert.

No matter how many times I said yes, I could not provide my patient with the care she needed. I had to come to grips with my inexperience, say no and refer her to a registered dietitian who was the expert. It was hard to swallow my pride. It was hard to realize I was defeated in my knowledge and my ability to care for a patient. Was it because I was not educated properly or did not remember every detail on how to care for someone with diabetes? Not at all. I realized this was not my flaw. I realized my flaw was not owning up to not providing the best education and not referring them out sooner. They needed more care than I could provide.

It is ok to say no. It is ok to not know everything. When we talked about judgement in Chapter 5, guess who is your biggest judge: you. We are our own worst critics and are the most hard on ourselves. As caretakers, we want to be able to provide everyone with everything they need. We need to keep growing and learning about our ever-evolving profession, but there are times when you just need to make the best decision for those we are helping.

2. Telling people what they want to hear.

We want our clients to feel warm and fuzzy when we are working with them, but sometimes we have to be sincere and honest. We want them to be successful and believe in what we bring to the table. Some of my most successful clients needed some tough love and it was difficult for me to provide. I did not want to be known as mean, but I also did not want to be know as a "softy" either.

There are times you have to say yes. Maybe for a particular client a fast food burger was ok in a certain situation. Then there are times when you say no. "No, you cannot eat a piece of cake the size of your head everyday. That is not beneficial for your health and will not meet your wellness goals." This might not be the approach you take, but, by being tactful in your presentation, your clients will resonate well with it and know you care.

Always remember, you are the expert and you know what your client needs. Being able to say yes and no when working with clients is better for them in the long run because you are caring for them the same way you would a member of your family.

3. Doing things for everyone else, without consideration of your needs.

When you say yes to others, make sure you are not saying no to yourself.
- Paulo Coehlo, Brazilian lyricist and novelist.

Then there is the fact that you are more than a registered dietitian. You have a life outside of your profession and it needs to be taken care of as well. If this very important part is not taken care of, you cannot be the best at your job. It is ok not to stay late and work on a project, if your family needs you. It is ok to take a mental health day, if you need a brain break. It is ok not to go to a meeting after work just because it is when it works for everyone else.

After many years of saying yes to everything at my job, I realized I was saying no to a lot in my personal life. I was skipping vacations because I did not want to create a bigger workload for my co-workers. I was staying late at work because someone else had to go to a family event, and, at the time, I was single and had a cat waiting at home. I would come in on weekends to make Monday easier on everyone. I would go to additional meetings or events no one else would volunteer for. I was trying to do it all and I quickly realized just couldn't do it anymore. It left me with minimal spare time to exercise, cook, see family and friends. It left me exhausted on the weekends and all I wanted to do was sleep. It was another contributing factor in leaving me not feeling excited about going to work anymore. I was missing out on all the good stuff. The "stuff" I worked for a paycheck to enjoy. I was missing out on "me" time. I was missing out on life.

I finally made the decision and gave myself permission to start saying no and not feeling one bit of remorse for it. Once I did, it became much easier to be happier at my job because I found the strength within myself to know my limits. Everything still got done at work. Meetings were attended, Monday still came and projects were completed. It's amazing how that happens. I wasn't exhausted anymore, my personal life was fulfilling and vacations were planned. I started to take care of me so I could better take care of my clients.

What are you doing to grow yourself in other ways? How are you feeding and nourishing your other interests?

This is necessary to your professional success and to continue enjoying your day or night job. This job is only a small part of you as a whole person. You must provide the other ingredients of you and choose the ripest, juiciest and sweetest ingredients you can find to make sure the recipe of you continues to be consistently made and remade. If you stop making a recipe, you stop because you lost the taste for it, it takes too much work and you have gotten lazy or you completely lost the recipe all together. It is so important to not lose the recipe of your happiness and success.

You are more than a registered dietitian, and, remember, you decide the best time to say yes. You also decide the best time to say no and you decide exactly what ingredients are the best for your professional and personal recipe that makes a balanced you.

You can do anything but not everything.
- David Allen, productivity consultant who is best known as the creator of the time management method known as "Getting Things Done".

Aligning Yourself

A balanced diet is a cookie in each hand.
- Unknown

Our profession is competitive. But who are we competitive with? Ironically, each other. It makes me sad to see this happen. While I was sitting in a meeting of registered dietitians from around the state, I have never seen an invisible line of separation more clearly. There was a distinct line of disconnect within a group of individuals who were all part of the same profession and who should be on the same team. During multiple discussion on this particular day, I got more and more heated inside because we were all there to be working toward the same goal, but instead, not all of us were on the same page. I have seen this happen too many times in a variety of registered dietitian situations and groups.

We are on the same team!

We need to start acting like it and treat each other as teammates.

As registered dietitians, we need to align yourself with other registered dietitians, and a variety of professionals and organizations who lift us up, not tear us down. By competing with other registered dietitians and not being a united front, we are degrading our profession and each other.

When thinking about your current role as a registered dietitian, there people or groups you have encountered who have either helped you achieve something or have been a resource for your success. In other words, partnerships. Everyone needs partnerships. Relationships between two or more persons who collaborate in a certain trade or business who contribute something substantial to the relationship. This can be expertise, money, resources or certain skills. Partnerships only enhance the current work you are doing by taking it to the next level.

When I think about my personal life, my initial and lifelong partnerships are my parents and other family members who have set the standard for my expectations of partners. Particularly, my parents are the two people who provided me with the resources to go to school, achieve my degree, as well as provide me with expertise on living a successful adult life. I would not be a registered dietitian without them and would not be able to enjoy or appreciate a comfortable life. I fashion my current and future partnerships to replicate the first and most important one of my life. My parents were also positive influencers in my life and lifted me up at all times. We are a team and continue to be a team, even if we do not agree on everything. We discuss and work through our differences and educate each other on those differences. Just because we do not see eye to eye on every detail, does not mean we will separate ourselves from our lifelong partnership.

Looking at my other current partnerships, I am lucky to have a great network of friends and family who are not registered dietitians and a network of friends who are registered dietitians. Each groups brings important expertise to the table. My non-registered dietitian friends work in all different aspects of life: business, marketing, investments, management, music, medicine, and education.

As registered dietitian, I tap into all of these resources because their expertise benefits me in many ways. When I have a question about how to educate a difficult client, I discuss teaching tactics with my friend in education. When I need information about a certain health condition, my medical friends step up to the plate. When I was considering starting my own consulting business, I had many conversations with my marketing, management and investing friends and family. My friend who is an expert in music, helped me learn how music helps my creativity and how to harness it into my work.

The best part of these partnerships is they share with others how they know a pretty great registered dietitian. They pass along my information to people they encounter in their own practices providing a referral process that keeps my business growing. By aligning myself with these individuals, I not only keep myself on the top of my game in my profession, but I create respected relationships leading to much more professional opportunities.

My registered dietitian partnerships are likewise very valuable. I am not an expert in all things nutrition as much as I would like to be. I try to keep up, but there is so much to know. A girl can only read so many articles and investigate so many studies. There are many different facets of nutrition because more and more registered dietitians are branching out from our conventional roles of clinical, community and food service.

By creating a network of registered dietitian experts whose expertise I value, in return, they inspire me to learn more from them and seek out situations to collaborate with them. Other registered dietitians are the perfect partners because we can support each other in many ways. No one else knows what we are going through professionally than another registered dietitian. I cannot talk to my non-registered dietitian partnerships about a client who doesn't want a low-sodium, lowfat diet education 10 hours after having open heart surgery. Or the client who wants to dine out for every meal but would like to lose 50 pounds in two months for an upcoming wedding she is in. You need to have other registered dietitians to talk about dietitian stuff with. This not only gives you resources in your profession but also gives you much needed dietitian sanity.

I want you to also consider being a willing partner for others. Put yourself out there for family, friends and other registered dietitians. Be available for questions and providing your expertise. By creating your team, you will be smarter and stronger for it. Be the best team player available to other registered dietitians. We do not share the same path, we do not have the same journey, but we have similar passions and we can be supportive at all times. I will never turn down another registered dietitian if something is asked of me and I will do anything to be a good partner. If I cannot help, I will share with them someone I know who will. This is what aligning yourself with the right people who enhance your life and career will do. It will also make it easier the next time you are sitting in a room with other registered dietitians, to encourage the team approach and be the teammates we desire and need in our profession.

When you're a part of a team, you stand up for your teammates. Your loyalty is to them. You protect them through good and bad, because they'd do the same for you.
- Yogi Berra, American professional baseball catcher, manager, and coach.

The Next Job or Jobs

Bread and water can easily be toast and tea.
- Unknown

I knew, in my heart, when it was time to move on to a new job. It was one of the hardest decisions I ever had to make. Because I do not make decisions quickly, deciding to take this job involved very fast decision making. I worked for a great company, I really loved my co-workers, and as you know from previous chapters, I was very comfortable in my job.

I had been at this job for seven years, my first job as a registered dietitian. I learned so much and I was grateful for the opportunity I was given right out of my internship. These people believed in me and gave me my first professional opportunity. Because I put a lot of stock into loyalty, I felt a pit in my stomach because I was worried I was going to let my co-workers down for considering another job (Hello! Caretaker!).

After I decided to accept my new job and believed I mustered up enough strength to tell my boss and co-workers the news, I found myself fighting back tears as I entered the building. I did not want to go to work to face the reality of the crazy change about to happen in my life. So I held off, for just a little longer. At the end of the day, when I could not clammer out of my office any faster and the feeling of unhappiness was strongly present, it clearly confirmed it was time for a change and I needed to tell them.

If you were to stand back and take a picture of your current job, what would you see?

By looking at the picture from afar, what do you feel?

Do you feel you're missing a few pieces of the puzzle?

Do you feel the puzzle is complete?

Take a long, hard look at the picture of what your professional life looks like. Do not be afraid to question what is happening in the picture. Ask people who are close to you what they see.

How you feel about your job is expressed in many different ways. You and other people will notice how you speak about your job. The energy you give to your job and the energy you give off while at work is something to analyze. Going through the motions, feelings of apathy, daydreaming about other things holding your interest may be signs you are in need of a career transformation.

For the last few years at my clinical job, I was browsing job openings for other professional options. I would not only check local ads, but national ads. I was looking not only for a new job, but new job opportunities in any geographical location. What other cool and amazing things were other registered dietitians doing that I may be missing out on? I found myself being envious of my peers for doing really kick ass things like working for a semi-professional football team, working as a nutrition consultant of a food company, and working for the Department of Education on programming for school nutrition. All of these jobs sounded more fascinating than what I was currently doing.

Do you find yourself being envious of other registered dietitians employed in other areas?

Do you fantasize about working in the jobs you find intriguing?

Towards the end, because I was very desperate for a change, I even thought about taking a break from being a registered dietitian all together. I was embracing thoughts of working in a completely different field to decrease the taxing effect it was having on my life. Fortunately, through the ups and downs of my sporadic emotions and thoughts, my passion remained strong enough to keep me vested in my chosen career.

I want to share with you a few things I realized when I was going through this range of open-ended career questions. At this time in my life, I really needed someone who knew what I was going through to discuss all these inquisitions with, but unfortunately, I ended up navigating it alone. When you are contemplating changing jobs, whether it is your second, third or tenth, I highly recommend considering the following thought provokers to help fill in the missing pieces of your professional puzzle and to find a mentor to converse with about your feelings towards your job:

1. **Make sure it is a job that is helping you grow professionally.**
   Make sure it is a job that brings new life and excitement into being a registered dietitian. Is it a job that continues to align with your passion and philosophy?

2. **Passion first. Pay Second.**
   I think many of us take jobs for the wrong reasons, money being the biggest influencer. Don't get me wrong, money is great and makes the world go around. At the end of the day, money's not everything. Most of us know and have come to terms with the fact that we are not going to become millionaires being a registered dietitian. This is why we have the passion and are truly drawn to what we are doing professionally as registered dietitians. When I left my first job, I did not get an increase in my pay or any additional benefits or perks. What made up for this was knowing the job more closely matched my passion. When I was making the decision to leave, I asked for an increase in my salary before I left to test the waters and to realize my commitment in needing a change. As a result, I was offered more money to stay. It was a revelation to sincerely know more money was just going to be a bandaid for what I was truly missing in my professional life. It would only have been a matter of time before the high wore off and the money was not enough to make me happy to stay in my job.

3. **Revisit your story and philosophy.**
   Really consider these when starting the job search. This was one thing I was not including into the equation when I initially started the

job hunt. I quickly realized, the perfect next job was not out there at the exact moment I needed and wanted it to be. In due time, the perfect next job was the one that was going to help me grow and help me live out and lead me to my truths as registered dietitian. By re-reading my story and philosophy, it guided me to the parameters I was looking for in the perfect job and what I needed professionally at this particular time in my life.

After you consider the above, it is also important to make some long term goals for yourself. After we graciously land our first job, most of us are not realistically thinking of our long term goals.

Where do I want to be in one year, five years, 10 years and how am I going to get there?

What is my plan?

Long term goals will match your passion and philosophy and can assist you when you are looking for future jobs. At the end of this section, take a few moments to question yourself on what your future professional life looks like. By doing so, you ensure you are constantly heading in the direction of a fulfilling career by the blueprint you have designed. Once you can answer these questions, I feel and hope you have a clearer picture of your professional long term goals. If you are struggling to answer these questions, now is probably not the time to set out on a job quest. It might be the right time to really dig deep, discover what you really want to be doing professional and designing the blueprint to get you there.

Because I started looking for jobs immediately when I felt the need for career change, nothing was really out there sparking my interest. What I wasn't really looking at was what really were my interests. When I took a step back and envisioned what I wanted my future to look like, things started to click. It took some time to work through my long term goals and it took a year to work through the three points above to truly understand the next steps I desired in my career. Shockingly, this is exactly when job opportunities presented themselves. I was ready and I understood what I was looking for.

Your profession is not what brings home your paycheck. Your profession is what you were put on Earth to do with such passion and such intensity that is becomes spiritual in calling.
- Vincent Van Gogh, a Dutch Post-Impressionist painter.

Now What? Worksheet

Exercise #1: Creating Your Philosophy

Who are you?

1. Write down 7 to 10 keywords describing who you are, and if I did an internet search for them, you would have a positive connection to the result or your name would pop up.

2. Write down 7 to 10 keywords that describe who you want to be as registered dietitian.

3. Do any of them match? Those matches will be keywords you will want to put into your philosophy and core values.

Why are You are a Registered Dietitian:

1. What is the purpose of nutrition?

2. What is your role as a registered dietitian?

3. What is it about dietetics that gives meaning to your life?

4. How do you see yourself influencing the profession of dietetics?

Your Audience:

1. Define the topics, nutritional concerns or types of clients you enjoy working with.

2. How will you reach and interact with the variety nutritional concerns, nutrition topics and types of clients you work with?

How Will You Perform:

1. What are your core beliefs as a registered dietitian? What clues or cues help you find the beliefs you feel deep down in your core? What information would you provide to your own family and friends?

2. How will your beliefs make you an effective registered dietitian?

3. How will you balance your beliefs with the beliefs and needs of your clients?

4. What are your goals for your clients?

5. What are your goals for your practice?

Your Professional Setting:

1. What gives you a sense of satisfaction at the end of the work day?

2. What type of environment feels most comfortable to be in (what do you think about doing and where do you want to be when you get up in the morning, what is the location).

3. Do you feel this is the right environment to work with others when it comes to the beliefs meaning the most to you?

4. Is this setting one that enhances your performance and excitement for being a registered dietitian?

Exercise #2: Creating Your Partnerships

Create this list and keep it handy when you need support in a particular area or you need expertise. An important part of this is to always be adding future partnerships.

1. Who are those people or groups who can help provide you with the information you need to advance your career and meet your goals?

2. Who are those people or groups who will share your passions and purpose?

3. Who are your future partners? Who are those people or groups you want to work and collaborate with?

Revisit your current and future partnership list every year as you evolve. Always be open to creating new connections and partnerships.

Exercise #3: Pre-Workout for Your Job Search

Here are a few questions to ask yourself to get you thinking about yourself and your professional wants:

1. What is my passion? (Hopefully you have already answered this!) What gets me fired up and what do I truly care about?

2. What are my past experiences? How do I feel about them?

3. What am I great at? My strengths? My weaknesses?

4. Where do I want to be? What abilities do I want to develop? What kind of registered dietitian do I want to become?

5. How am I going to become the registered dietitian I want to be? What resources do I need? How am I going to find them?

6. What is stopping me or holding me back from what I want to do professionally?

7. From whom can I learn the most? Who can teach me and give me the knowledge I need to become this kind of registered dietitian?

Part Three:

What is Your Superpower?

Sometimes you have to be your own hero.

Eleven

Being a Mentor and a Role Model

*Strength is the capacity to break a chocolate bar into four pieces with your
bare hands-and then eat just one of the pieces.*
- Judith Viorst, American writer, newspaper journalist,
and psychoanalysis researcher.

I bet if I asked if you remembered any of your preceptors or mentors while

going through college or your internship, you would instantly have a mental picture of a few pretty stellar people who made an impact on your life. Just for a second, think about all they did for your development as a registered dietitian. Think of what you learned, think of the time and energy they spent with you, think of how you felt about them as a registered dietitian during this time. What did you learn from them? How did they make you feel when you worked with them? Did you want to fashion your career after them? Did they share anything with you that has made you the registered dietitian you are today?

When I look back on my undergrad, internship and my jobs, I realized there is so much more to be a registered dietitian than just working. There is much dedication by our peers to educate and grow future registered dietitians. I can honestly and wholeheartedly say, I loved all my preceptors when I was in my internship. I learned an infinite amount of quality information from all of them and find myself still using their expertise today in my practice.

After being an intern at my first place of employment, I was fortunate to become a preceptor myself. At the time, being so new in the profession, I did not feel I was suitable to be a preceptor because I still felt I had much to learn. Why in the world would they allow me to be a preceptor for someone who was just one year behind me in my journey? Looking back, I realized it did make sense. Having a variety in years of experience gives future registered dietitians great exposure to the different stages in our journeys. Interns really need this and interns really want this. I wanted it. I wanted to know different perspectives of a registered dietitian one year out, five years out, or even more.

After the first intern I worked with, I realized how our profession really needs to pay it forward. It is one of the most beautiful and inspiring things about being a registered dietitian. We value ourselves and our future practitioners. We want and expect our legacies to be the best damn registered dietitians practicing in this world. The next few times I was a preceptor, it became easier and more rewarding. I learned this was an important part of my career and it left me wanting to do more mentoring.

Being a mentor and role model for future dietitians has been the key to my successes and even some of my failures. When I was stuck in a rut and wanting something more, being a preceptor kept me in the game because it was providing a different dimension to my job. It added spice and flavor each day that was otherwise very vanilla and bland. I have been able to learn from those I have mentored even more than I have probably given them because they have enhanced my own skill set.

During the process of being a preceptor, I committed my interns to three things I expected and hoped for them during their journey:

1. Always strive to do the best you can in any situation you are put into
2. Ask questions when you have them
3. Have fun!

These 3 things resonated with my interns.. I have walked in their shoes and remember what it was like to be an intern. I also remember comparing stories with other interns in my class and quickly realized I was one lucky gal with my positive experiences. I could not believe what some of my peers were going through during their rotations: anywhere from only cleaning dishes during Food Service Management to just handing out checks to WIC clients. This were not learning experiences, but something more along the lines of doing tasks no one else wanted to do.

The internship should be the biggest and most fruitful way to learn about what kind of registered dietitian you want to be, not learning about running a large dishwasher in a hospital kitchen. I cannot tell you how many times I have heard from interns and new dietitians that they questioned continuing in our field because of preceptors who really did not care. They did not care about teaching and definitely did not care about the profession. Where was their passion? Where was their purpose?

When you are a mentor, you foster insight and expand growth opportunities. You foster not only their professional growth, but your own as well. These experiences have to be viewed as a learning experience for both entities. I know I am the registered dietitian today because of my preceptors and mentors. It is unbelievable to be that I can reach out to my previous preceptors at anytime because we have stayed in contact and they are permanently engraved on my partnership list.

One of my preceptors, Brenda, has become one of my dearest and closest friends, and ironically, one of the registered dietitians I was a preceptor for, Amanda, is also one of my dearest and closest friends. We would have never developed these friendships if it was not for dietetics. We would have never connected the way we did without having positive experiences, on both ends, during an internship.

I know many of you may feel taking on mentoring or being a preceptor can complicate or slow down the work day for you. Or to put it in simpler terms: you just do not have time. Precious and limited time. There is absolutely no value you can put on investing time into future registered dietitians. It is priceless.

As a preceptor, I did value my time and a couple of interns who came across my path made me question why I was investing my time into them. I was completely appalled they did not have the same passion and dedication as I did to their internship. It pissed me off. These people beat out other candidates who really wanted to be registered dietitians. Why were they wasting their time and mine? Why did they enter into something I held in the highest of importance? I had a very important learning moment: not all dietetic interns should be interns and future registered dietitians. So how would I, as a preceptor, help navigate this situation for myself and the intern? At first, it was quit being a preceptor, problem solved. I went through an entire year without being a preceptor. It was one of the worst decisions I had made.

Because I had worked with interns who were passionate about being a registered dietitian and worked with interns who were not in it to win it, my need for paying it forward became strongly apparent. I needed the interactions with aspiring registered dietitians; the teaching, the learning and the relationship. I needed the challenges of interns who were not 100% on board with our profession and help them find their passion or discover where their passions really were. I needed to share my journey.

I will never claim to be perfect and I tell my interns this on the first day. I might cuss a little, I might have to work through things by talking to myself, I might be a little disorganized, and there is a good chance I might not know the answers to their questions, but I will find out. What I do know is I love being a registered dietitian. I love sharing my journey. I love being a preceptor and a mentor. I want them to see the human side of being a registered dietitian and everything going along with it. I want them to know the truth. I want them to work hard and to have fun. Most of all, I want them to feel the warm and fuzzy feelings about their future career like I do.

I love seeing my past interns and hearing about their successes. There is nothing as rewarding as having a tiny part in their passions coming alive. It also builds a network of resources benefitting both of us. These registered dietitians are working in jobs I can build partnerships with. Somewhere down the road, we may need each other's expertise and we have this resource in our tool belt.

There is nothing that makes me more ecstatic than reconnecting with the numerous registered dietitians I have had the joy to work with early in their careers. I am forever grateful my preceptors gracefully offered up their time and the commitment to my success. They did it because they wanted to, they did it because they value our profession. They did it because they care.

This profession would not exist without preceptors, mentors and role models. Slowly, this pool of experts offering their time is dwindling. Please consider being a registered dietitian who is willing to teach, to care, to comfort and to be a resource for future and current registered dietitians. If it is only a week, a month, or a year, anytime you offer to our future will pay you back twofold.

If you are in the pre-contemplation or contemplation stage, I strongly encourage you to take 10 minutes and watch this TED Talk featuring Karen Russell that you might find a little inspiring. Modern Mentoring: The Good, The Bad and The Better: https://www.youtube.com/watch?v=SSZRtx8m3Z8

The Academy of Nutrition and Dietetics is also a great resource for information on mentoring. They are building a great online community for mentors in our profession and you can find more information at the end of the book.

If you are interested in being a preceptor, I recommend reaching out to a local college or university with a dietetic or didactic program and offer your expertise to their students. Remember to consider it an opportunity to educate others but to also educate yourself. If you have been in the field for a while, it is a great way to learn what is on the forefront of dietetics, how current students are learning and what they want to learn.

Being a mentor also gives you the ability to develop and possibly retain future employees for your organization. I try to take an intern or work with a student at least once a year. I have had the joy of employing two dietetic students over the course of four years. Alysse and Erin renewed my excitement again and they worked fantastically within our organization. We talked about what is being taught in their classes and they shared with me the things that have changed since I was in their shoes. I offered training, education and a sounding board for their questions of all things dietetics. And as the proud "mama bear" registered dietitian that I am, both of them applied and were accepted into internships. The rest is history!

Being a preceptor and mentor is much more rewarding than anything I have accomplished so far in my years of being a registered dietitian. The best part is those I have mentored, will in turn be mentors too. I am part of their journey and they are part of mine. It feels great to know I have created a network of registered dietitians who will support each other and continue a legacy that started with my own incredible preceptors.

The heart of mentoring: Getting the most out of life is not about how much you keep for yourself, but how much you pour into others.
- David Stoddard, Author and mentor.

Twelve

Be the Face of Nutrition

The same boiling water that softens the potato hardens the egg.
It's about what you're made of. Not the circumstances.
- Unknown

Putting yourself out there for all the world see and hear is not something registered dietitians do. We tend to lean on the conservative side and do not toot our own horns often enough for the incredible things we are doing. When it comes down to it, we are changing and saving lives. Hell yeah, we are! If this alone does not warrant a million horns going off daily, then I don't know what does.

The caretakers in us are more focused on those we serve and the process of of doing the best at our jobs. Often, we lose sight of spreading the message of how important we are in this world. The expectations we have from others and the pressure we put on ourselves is very rigorous. Sometimes, we do not want to take off our registered dietitian hats and just be ourselves for a few moments. There are moments we want to fade into the background, not have anyone know this is our job, eat an extra large hot fudge sundae at the local ice cream shop and not be known as a registered dietitian. Unfortunately, this usually does not work in our world or in our profession.

When I think about the hardest part of our job, it is not about being a good educator, saving lives, managing a budget, or meeting a deadline. It is about being recognized and known as the nutrition expert.

People know who their Doctor is, people know who their Dentist is, but do people know who their Dietitian is?

When I discussed our competition earlier in Chapter Five the reason was to provide you with ways to set ourselves apart from the others who do not have our credentials. These are things we can do separate us, but there is one far more important: being the face of nutrition.

What do I mean by this? Well, I challenge you to look into a mirror and take a good long look at your beautiful face, the thing sitting on the top of your shoulders at the front of your head. This is what people recognize. This is what people will correlate with how they know you. Maybe they saw you in an article, maybe they saw you at a presentation, maybe they were your patient in a hospital, or a child who recognized you from their school lunch room. The point being, a person might not remember your name, but they will almost always recognize your face.

Think of where you live and your neighborhood. Even if you do not personally know your neighbors, they will recognize you as the person who lives in the white house on the corner, the person who drives the blue car, or the neighbor down the street who walks their golden retriever every evening. They are comfortable with you, wave as you drive down the street or when you are walking your dog. You are approachable for a small conversation or maybe sharing a cocktail on your patio during the summer.

Where you work is also your neighborhood. People in this neighborhood will also recognize you, wave and talk with you. They will invite you to events and ask your opinion or interest in different things because they know who you are and what you do. I think it is so important to cultivate and nourish this neighborhood as well.

I am recognized as a registered dietitian in all of my "neighborhoods." Denise, who comes to my grocery store to shop, recognizes me and calls me her dietitian. The kids I work with at the local elementary school call me Miss Anne, the lady who comes to their school to teach them about nutrition and brings them snacks. A local group I do cooking classes with calls me their "Chef Dietitian."

Non-verbal communication is an important key to being an effective communicator. Facial expressions, movements of your body, gestures and eye contact are all key components to how you communicate with others. Albert Mehrabian, a psychologist, concluded this in a non-verbal communication study and silent messaging to others: "Total Liking = 7% Verbal Liking + 38% Vocal Liking + 55% Facial Liking." 55% likability of your beautiful face is a key factor in developing and building your brand, enhancing connections and recognition as the nutrition expert.

When I was working in my first job, there was not comradery of my team wanting to be the face of nutrition. We kind of worked in the shadows and did our jobs hoping to be recognized when needed. I do believe there was some desire to be recognized by physicians and called upon by them for our expertise. However, we did not have the time or the resources to develop those relationships because we did not have the support from upper management to aid in the effort into making it happen. Our focus was to do our jobs well, whether we were recognized and if our services were requested or not.

When I started my second job, it was a complete 180. I was required to get a professional headshot, and my face was plastered on posters, signs, emails, pamphlets and handouts. At the time, I can't say it was my most favorite part of my job, but a light bulb went off and it all completely made sense. My face was the best marketing tool available to my neighborhoods and to build rapport with my customers.

Looking back on my first job, if our "marketing" was handled similarly to my retail dietitian job, I feel our colleagues and physicians would have been more aware of our presence and expertise. They would read our chart notes, recognize our names and use our recommendations for our patients. Other professionals in the hospital would also be more willing to refer and consult with us for nutrition related needs. It would have advanced the importance of our role in the healthcare team.

You do not have to own your own business to be the face of nutrition. Any registered dietitian in any job can do this. You can be the face of nutrition in schools and universities, hospitals, public health and education departments, government, retail, fitness arenas, extension, media, and as any member of any community. As a registered dietitian in the here and now, whenever I am a guest blogger or write an article for a column in a newspaper or magazine, I include my headshot. Whenever I do a presentation, I include my headshot with my biography. I have business cards with my face on them. My face is my best marketing tool because it is with me all the time, it is my walking billboard and brand. It is me, I am a nutrition expert and I am proud as hell of that.

Over the years, I have been able to put together a simple and effective "Be the Face of Nutrition" toolbox. These are the easy ideas I feel work well to carry out this important concept we should be incorporating into our jobs and everyday lives.

When you put together this easy toolbox, you are creating a consistent message of being the face of nutrition and being the nutrition expert. The key word is consistent. Be as consistent with your written messaging as you are with your public presence so people always know that YOU are THEIR registered dietitian. This should be an easy thing to do. Pick one if that works for you or pick all three. I hope you will include this in your superhero utility belt to not only help yourself become more recognizable as the nutrition expert but to continue the movement and advancement of all registered dietitians.

Your smile is your logo, your personality is your business card, how you leave others feeling after having an experience with you is your trademark.
- Jay Danzie, Author.

Thirteen

Be Great. Always

In cooking, you have to be able to master something good
before you can make something great.
- Katie King Mumford, Graphic Designer and Cook.

There are many times in our careers as registered dietitians, we question ourselves and if we are doing a "good" job. Whether it was a complicated nutrition question, a patient we worked with that was not a successful partnership, a recipe that did not taste good, an issue with an employee or coworker, a budget discrepancy or a presentation that did not go well. All I can say is: sh*% happens. As much as we strive to do everything well, we cannot be perfect all the time.

Anyone can be a good registered dietitian. Being good at our profession is desirable and safe. Begin a good registered dietitian is fantastic. But being a good registered dietitian is not being a great registered dietitian. I knew I was a good registered dietitian, but something inside me was always clouding my mind.

How good am I really?

Am I giving my profession and myself everything I can?

I felt I was not making strides or making the shift to being more than good. My heart and mind knew there was so much more I wanted, and good was no longer appealing to me. I needed to make things happen. I needed to find greatness in everything I was doing and surround myself with people who inspire me to do more and be great.

For long term greatness in your career and maintaining life-work balance, It is important to sometimes go the extra mile and to take a few steps back and think outside of the box. As registered dietitians, we are defined to fit into certain roles and do certain jobs. We are given "parameters" to fit a job description in the places we work. We take on many different things but never really focus on the things that are truly importance to each of us. Because our jobs have certain requirements, sometimes it takes all we have to give by completing those parameters daily.

Where is the time for us to work on greatness and not always just doing the acceptable good?

This is exactly when we lose interest, lose faith in our profession and ourselves and consider a job change. This moment is when we might decide dietetics is not for us. This moment is when we need to continue to have high expectations of ourselves, keep believing in what we want to achieve and revisit the action plan of our passion.

Why did we become registered dietitians in the first place?

The beautiful world of nutrition and dietetics has endless opportunities for us to find our greatness. There is no time like the present to seek and find fulfilling greatness in your professional life. You need to dream big of what you want to do and go for it.

What is the action plan to achieve the goals and greatness you desire?

As satisfying the good was in my life, I wanted more. In the beginning stages of my career, I loved my job and rarely had days I did not want to go. I was pushing myself and working hard. Repetition, similarity and monotony set in, the days of not looking forward to work started happening and I slowly stopped being true to myself. I was no longer giving the job my all and had many moments of daydreaming for the excitement I felt in the infancy of my job.

Greatness has nothing to do with being better than anyone and has everything to do with being the best version of you.

A couple of years ago, I was at a conference with a group of registered dietitians and we were separated into small groups. The leader of the group suggested we go around the room, tell everyone our jobs and something that was on our bucket list. As we went around the room, almost every registered dietitian shared their name and current job in the least passionate way. There was not one ounce of excitement about their jobs in a room of 30+ dietitians. All I could think was how was this possible? How could an entire group of my peers stoically shared their job without one bit of spark?

When it was time to share what was on their bucket list, eyes brightened, postures straightened and their whole demeanor changed. Their passion was not in their career, instead, their passion was everywhere and anywhere else. This was an awakening moment to me. I had to create and find inspiration in my life to keep the fire going. I had to dig deep into my passion and philosophy and finds ways to recreate the vision I had for myself and my career.

No one is born great, but greatness happens with the effort and focus given to what you are passionate about. I had to find greatness. I wanted my career and my bucket list to show the same kind of spark and excitement when I talked about both.

How can we combine all the things we want to do in life and in our career with all the things we are obligated to do?

I find greatness in being a registered dietitian who does not only focus on my day to day job, but all the other things I do as registered dietitian. There is Anne, the retail registered dietitian, and there is Anne, the registered dietitian who writes books, is a guest blogger, develops recipes, is a leader, volunteers to work with kids. For me, being great is giving everything I am passionate about my all. I am willing to take risks; I am accepting of failure; I am open to experiencing what life has to offer. I am so passionate about being a registered dietitian and in return, helping other registered dietitians succeed is empowering. I find in my pursuit of greatness, I am being 100% true to myself and not settling for less than I deserve. This is why I do what I do.

My job makes me good. My professional choices and the people I surround myself with, make me great. I need more in my life than just a 9-to-5 job. I need to have other nutrition and wellness interests which make me grow and fulfill my life. I have had to give up things and people in my life because they were no longer appealing to me. Letting go of this part of my life and what I thought in my mind was good, was the hardest part. It was also the best part. It opened me up to seeking out other possibilities our profession provides. We do not have to be the cookie cutter registered dietitian in community nutrition, food service or clinical nutrition. There are so many other great opportunities out there just waiting for each of us.

You and only you can define what greatness means in your life. You are a good registered dietitian, I am positive of this. It is time to believe in yourself and open yourself up to new challenges encouraging your devotion to being a registered dietitian for a long time.

Do you feel you are fulfilling the greatness inside of you? Is there something you have always wanted to do, something that is calling you but you're holding back? Are you opening yourself up to all that life have to offer?

If you feel this way, even in the tiniest bit, it is time to start making the shift. There is always something that will hold you back. Whether it's time, money, family, and an overall sense of responsibility you feel for the life you live. Remember, you are also responsible for you and your happiness. When you take yourself out of the equation, life will get long and your passion will fade. Then being a registered dietitian turns into a job and not a true passion anymore.

I have been there, you have been there, or you might find yourself at this point in life. Because I have questioned wanting to continue my career as a dietitian many time, by choosing greatness in everything I do, has rejuvenated my passion and desire to be in this field. I also have a clearer understanding of what I need outside of my job to keep myself interested and prospering in my job. I gave up the good and went for the great. I will never look back.

Don't be afraid to give up the good to go for the great.
- John D. Rockefeller, an American industrialist and philanthropist.

Fourteen

Leadership

I'm a leader, not a follower. Unless it's a dark place, then you're going first.

- Anonymous

Part of the registered dietitian journey is discovering new aspects of our profession. Many of us are so focused on our jobs and personal lives, we forget about the numerous registered dietitians who volunteer their time to support the advancement and relevancy of the profession as the nutrition expert.

This is something I did not know anything about when I was working in my first job. I was not educated in my internship about how our profession has a national dietetics organization and each state has an affiliate dietetic association that is comprised of registered dietitians from all around the state practicing in all different areas of our profession. Some people are willfully employed by these organizations but the majority of them are volunteers. Eight years of being a registered dietitian and I had no idea about any of this. How was this possible?

Why wasn't there more conversation of interest and desire to be active in groups who support registered dietitians?

When I moved to Iowa and started working in retail, one of my supervisors who was in a leadership position as the Marketing Chair with the Iowa Academy of Nutrition and Dietetics (formerly known as the Iowa Dietetic Association), needed to pass the torch to someone else because of time constraints. She asked for volunteers who may be interested in taking over her role. As she spoke about the position, I instantly became interested. I thought it would be a great opportunity to get to know what my affiliate was about, as well as volunteering my time.

When this opening presented itself, I had been at my retail job for a few years now. Guess what? I was starting to feel a little restless, lazy, unmotivated and too settled in my current routine. This was just the kick in the ass I needed to refocus and work on my greatness. I accepted the leadership role and became the Marketing Co-Chair for the Iowa Academy. For three years, I was introduced to a completely different side of our profession.

Being a part of this group introduced me to new people who were doing exciting things as registered dietitians. I learned about jobs I had no idea existed, I found myself among vast cumulative years of experience and expertise. This was a gift I was given to gain confidence in the workforce as a registered dietitian and network with others who are inspiring.

I learned valuable leadership skills by working with a harmonious team by brainstorming, negotiating, creating, communicating and problem solving. It was exciting and scary all at the same time because it was new to me, and I also felt like I had no idea what I was doing.

That is the great thing about volunteering and leadership. It is ok if you do not know what you are doing. The people you work with want to help you learn and succeed. Doesn't this sound very familiar to your time as an intern?

In my experience with the Iowa Academy, if you bring the passion and the devotion, they bring the support and the pom poms. Seriously, what a great family to be a part of! I learned more about the function and importance of the Academy of Nutrition and Dietetics, the Iowa Academy and the support they provide their members. There is a need for these groups to help keep our profession relevant to our state and our nation, and these groups need you.

The fascinating part of my journey was finding the leader in myself I never knew existed. As a leader, I am able to express my strong beliefs about the future of our profession, live out and share the deep passions I have, build up others along their journey and be part of a team with a similar vision. Most importantly, I was able to use my ideas and influences to serve others. I started out as Marketing Co-Chair, which lead to President-Elect, President and currently, Immediate Past President.

When I started in marketing, we worked on the Kids Eat Right Campaign and successfully made Iowa one of the leaders in volunteers across the country. In following years, we switched the focus on increasing the awareness of the registered dietitian being the nutrition expert in the the State of Iowa, supporting our membership and increasing advocacy. This has been the lead focus ever since. As a leader and volunteer, I was a part of creating a driving vision for the future in collaborating on a strategic plan to execute this.

Since then, a successful marketing campaign has been in place and we build upon it each year in our strategic plan. Many calls to action have lead to advocacy, growing partnerships, media presence and public awareness of registered dietitians being the real nutrition experts Iowans should be searching for with nutrition needs. We developed a media spokespersons group to increase public awareness and have streamlined our messaging with monthly themes, blog, social media and television appearances with local news stations throughout the state.

I traveled to Washington DC and learned about advocacy and legislation affecting registered dietitians. I worked alongside our Public Policy and State Legislative Coordinators and others interested in policy by speaking with our national Senators and Representatives. I did not think I had an interest in policy until I saw the passion from so many registered dietitians from around the country.

I was also fortunate to collaborate with the other leadership and groups in my affiliate on the process of creating, publishing and marketing a professional and admirable nutrition resource sold all over the country known as our Simplified Diet Manual. All of this is happened because people came together with similar passions and purpose for the advancement of our profession. I take a step back, inhale a deep breath and smile because I am so grateful to be a part of all of this.

This experience has been beyond beneficial for me to surround myself with other registered dietitians flourishing in dietetics, flourishing in their lives and being exposed to the different stages of their unique journeys. The accessibility to different minds, passions, purposes invigorates me. I am aware of great things my 900+ peers in Iowa are doing and accomplishing. It gives me confidence in knowing I am doing great things too. Working with like-minded registered dietitians for the same company or business is supportive, understanding and empowering. But it can all be too similar and stagnant. If you feel the same way about where you are now, needing a little spark of variety, it might be time to give volunteering and leadership a try.

Do you have an interest in being a leader? Do you know how to get active with your local dietetic or district groups? Have you ever been a part of leadership for your affiliate? If so, has it been awhile since you have been active?

I challenge you to ask yourself these questions. When we cannot change our demographics or our employment, this is a perfect way to reinvent ourselves and ignite our passion in different ways.

I will not sugar coat anything (as much as I love sugar): Leadership has a lot of responsibility with a lot of hard work involved but it does not come without joy. I was willingly representing over 900 registered dietitians in my state, and of course, I was not going to let anyone down. When I took the challenge of leadership, I was going to put my whole heart and soul into doing the best job I could. I made decisions I felt were in the best interest of our members and affiliate, and I leave behind a legacy I am proud of. I am proud of all we accomplished as a team and I look forward to all we are going to accomplish in the future. Younger registered dietitians are showing interest in volunteering and leadership in our organization. We are also invigorating current registered dietitians to revisit leadership.

At the end of the day, you will never regret volunteering your time to support our profession. With passion there is pain, and, at times, I struggled with some decision making. I struggled with leadership/volunteering/work/life balance, but it has all been worth it because it isn't just about me. It is about something greater and bigger than me. It is about the 900 members of nutrition experts in Iowa who are the best registered dietitians in the nation. I cannot wait to continue this part of my journey with them.

You must be the change you wish to see in the world.
- Mahatma Gandhi, the preeminent leader of the Indian nationalism in British-ruled India.

Fifteen

Your Future and the Future of Dietetics

*"When you wake up in the morning, Pooh," said Piglet at last,
"what's the first thing you say to yourself?"
"What's for breakfast?" said Pooh. "What do you say, Piglet?"
"I say, I wonder what's going to happen exciting today?" said Piglet.
Pooh nodded thoughtfully. "It's the same thing," he said."*
- A.A. Milne, an English author, best known for his books about the
teddy bear Winnie-the-Pooh and for various poems.

With the increasing interest of the role nutrition has in everyone's lives, our future looks very bright and robust. Preventative healthcare is becoming more of the norm by lessening the effect of growing healthcare costs.

The health and wellness desires of our population is encouraging more facets of the importance of nutrition. We are investing in our youth by working toward healthier food programs and increasing nutrition and physical education in schools. Business and employers are taking notice because healthier employees equals better performance. Medical facilities, insurance companies, government programs, legislation, public health, universities, and the average human are realizing being proactive with health and wellness is the key to living a longer and healthier life.

A few things come to light when we think about the evolving nutrition landscape. One, obesity is affecting more than one third of our nation's population which is a precursor for other major diseases. Two, the Baby Boomer generation is growing older and looking to be healthier to live longer lives. Three, the younger generations, Generation X, Millenials/Generation Y and Generation Z, really care about food. These generations like to be a part of something and specific food preferences gives them an identity and the ability to align themselves with a particular group. These groups include food allergies, vegetarians, vegans, gluten free, raw, and numerous other types of eating preferences. These "tribes" want to know where their food comes from, what is it made of and the role it plays in their personal health and wellness journey.

In the nutrition landscape, it is also important to address the emerging biohacker or personalized nutrition food tribe. This tribe consists of our prospective clients who wear technology to track fitness, calories and sleep. They are looking for science-based evidence of their health needs through blood tests, DNA samples, urine and stool samples to see what is going on in their bodies to understand and know how and what to eat for optimum health.

All of these people need us. All of these people need to be seeking out a registered dietitian to provide them with the most sound and accurate nutrition information. All registered dietitians need to be informed and educated on the emerging changes to the nutrition landscape.

In 2012, The US Bureau of Labor and Statistics, provided these statistics relating to registered dietitians and registered dietitian nutritionists. Employment of dietitians and nutritionists are projected to grow 21% from 2012 to 2022. In 2012, there were 67,400 job available. That is predicting an increase of around 14,000 jobs over 10 years. The average growth of most professions is around 14 percent. This makes our profession's growth 6 percent faster than the national average.

The workforce is becoming more and more diverse for our profession. We are not strictly held to the standard definitions of food service, community and clinical nutrition. Registered dietitians are working in corporate wellness programs, schools (incorporating speciality diets, nutrition education in the classroom and innovative recipes to meet strict school nutrition guidelines), culinary experts and chefs, speciality areas such as food allergies and sports nutrition, supermarkets, technology-based businesses, research, natural food companies, mainstream food companies, clinicians with private practice, medical teams and the list goes on.

The future is ours, if we are ready and prepared to offer what it needs. Think back to the chapter in which I discussed our competition. If we are not ready for what is needed, our profession is going to lose out to those who are ready. We do not want our competition to take those 14,000 jobs that are ours for the taking. We also want to be the ones creating additional jobs based on what people need and want. We have to keep setting ourselves apart as the nutrition experts.

To keep us moving forward, recall the other key ingredients in our registered dietitian recipe: being a mentor, being the face of nutrition, being a nutrition expert by communicating health messages in your community, having your expertise be available to the millions of hungry people looking for it through all types of media and having a vision of where you want our profession to be. Think of ways a registered dietitian will benefit in all areas of life and share them with other registered dietitians and professionals. Do not be afraid to approach a business or company with how employing a registered dietitian would benefit them. Offer them a "taste" of what you have to offer, a lecture, a special class, research of interest to you and them, maybe even a wellness consultation with a CEO. Nothing you ever imagine or devise is a failure if you are innovative. Businesses of all types, shapes and sizes are on a wellness journey of their own. If there is not an immediate need, they will remember you and your dazzling face of nutrition expertise, and will contact you when they are ready.

If you don't see the book you want on the shelf, write it.
- Beverly Cleary, American writer of children's and young adult fiction.

Sixteen

What Do You Want to Be When You Grow Up?

First we eat then we do everything else.
- M.F.K. Fisher, a preeminent American food writer.

Do you remember the first job you ever had way before you became a registered dietitian? Did you believe you would work there for the rest of your adult life? Of course not. Your life is about experiencing different jobs and learning what you like and don't like. Not all jobs are a great fit. Some jobs are tolerable because you know at the time it is something you have to do. When you were in college, you sought out nutrition-related jobs and volunteer positions to get experience to build your resume and for securing an internship. For one day, I worked at a nursing home as a nutrition assistant. I was excited and hopeful for this position, until I realized my job consisted of setting up for breakfast and lunch dinner service, followed by cleaning dishes.

How was this job going to give me the experience I needed to be a registered dietitian?

Immediately, I knew this was not the job for me. I knew I needed the experience, but I also knew this job was not going to be a bullet point on my resume. The next morning, I tearfully walked into the office of the registered dietitian who hired me and told her the job was not the right fit for me. I honestly told her my heart was not into it and I would not be able to give 100% effort 100% of the time. Surprisingly, she was very understanding and told me she knew exactly where I was coming from.

To this day, this was the only job I ever quit that I felt horrible doing so. At the time, I felt I let my boss down. When in reality, I really let myself down for applying, accepting and not committing to a job deemed "important" for my dietetic future. As I drove away that day, I decided I was not going apply to work somewhere I could not give my all to. If my heart and dedication was not there from day one, it would not be there on day 30. In this situation, I knew I needed the experience, but I needed to find it in different ways.

When we first start out, all we want is a job. It is hard because so many jobs require experience. Once we land our first one (woo hoo!), we feel we are so lucky to even have it. We are very excited about being a registered dietitian we immediately want to start working and practicing. You may discover after working at your first job for some time, you might find you really like it. It is helping you grow, you are excited to be there and you feel you are living out your passion. But as you change and your purpose changes, you may realize this job is not quite the right fit and you keep working and doing your duties. You don't hate the job, it is paying the bills and it is stable. There are good benefits, you like the people you work with and the drive is short and close to home. When people ask you how your job is going, you respond with "fine" and everything is status quo.

Where is the excitement you had when you first started? Where is the excitement when you are at work? Is there anything giving you joy when you are there?

Not many of us stay at our first job for our entire professional career. If you have, that is wonderful! I would love to talk with you, so you can share your success with living out your passion from the start. The average worker stays at his or hers job for around four years according to the Bureau of Labor and Statistics and this is decreasing as our job force is getting younger. If this statistic is true, most people will have more than 15 different jobs in their lifetime. Why do you think this is happening? Because people do not want to be stuck in a rut. People have passions and purpose and want to be fulfilled in their jobs. By having different jobs, people realize what they find interesting and what matches their passions by experiencing different roles and learning different skill sets along the way.

Registered dietitians are a group of professionals who like to stay comfortable. We like to stick with what we know because it is safe. Many of us have been practicing for a while and know great jobs are sometimes hard to come by. We also are not as familiar with the new and advancing job market for registered dietitians. With the creation of new job opportunities, we do not have to stay in a particular job because of limited options available.

Dietetics is a career blossoming into a profession where we can create our own path. We can use our credentials to cross over into other job titles - sometimes some additional schooling is needed. Here are a few examples: Health Coach, Food Specialist, Food Scientist, Wellness Coordinator,

Nutrition Researcher, Recipe Developer, Nutrition Analysis Expert, Food Labeling Specialist, Supermarket Dietitian, Health/Nutrition Coordinator, and Nutrition Marketing Partner.

To advance your career and hone your passion into a specific area of nutrition expertise, there are numerous opportunities to specialize in. Below are various listings of offerings we can explore to advancing our career. Please refer to my resources and reference pages for more information.

The Commision on Dietetic Registration offers these Board Certified Specialties in Nutrition: Pediatric, Oncology, Sport, Gerontology, Renal Certificates of Training in Adult and Childhood and Adolescent Weight Management and Advanced Practice Certification in Clinical Nutrition.

The American Society of Parenteral and Enteral Nutrition (ASPEN) offers the Certified Nutrition Support Clinician®.

The National Certification Board for Diabetes Educators (NSBCE) offers the Certified Diabetes Educator® (CDE®).

The American Association of Diabetes Educators offers Diabetes Prevention Program Lifestyle Coach Training (LSC) to acquire the necessary skills to deliver a successful National Diabetes Prevention Program (DPP) based on the curriculum developed by the Centers for Disease Control and Prevention (CDC).

If you have an interest in food allergies/sensitivities, you may want to consider becoming a Certified Lifestyle Eating and Performance (LEAP) Therapist (CLT) through Signet Diagnostic. There are mentors available for you to discuss if the certification is right for you.

Functional and integrative health is on the rise. There are a few avenues available for additional education and certification. Certification as a Functional Medicine Practitioner is available through the Institute for Functional Medicine. This program is the top certification of the functional medicine world. Because they are very selective in who takes their course, you must apply to be considered for entering this certification program. This program deems Registered Dietitians as candidates for their

program, along with medical doctors, nurse practitioners, nurses, dentists and pharmacists.

The Integrative and Functional Nutrition Academy certification program is an online course founded by registered dietitians, and when completed, you will be an Integrative and Functional Nutrition Certified Practitioner™ (IFNCP™). This is open to all health professionals, but primarily is for registered dietitians.

Next Level Functional Nutrition is also integrative functional medical nutrition therapy certificate program created by a registered dietitian open to all health professionals. This certificate program also has a culinary option you can include in your training.

If you work in Food Service Management and are looking to specialize, the National Restaurant Association offers the Foodservice Management Professional® (FMP®) certification.

For opportunities in fitness and health coaching, I recommend visiting the American Council on Exercise (ACE). ACE offers a variety of certifications in fitness and is the only Health Coach Certification program accredited by the National Commission for Certifying Agencies (NCCA).
The Academy of Nutrition and Dietetics offers Certificates of Training in the following:

- Advancing Your Role as Leader
- Chronic Kidney Disease Nutrition Management
- Developing Your Role as Leader
- Executive Management
- Food Allergies: Cutting Through the Clutter
- Nutritional Counseling
- Restaurant Menu Labeling: The Impact on the Environment of Nutrition and Dietetics

- Supermarket Business and Industry Skills to Thrive in Retail Dietetics
- Vegetarian Nutrition
- Training in Adult Malnutrition
- Culinary Nutrition

The Academy of Nutrition and Dietetics also has Dietetic Practice Groups for their members which are professional-interest groups. These groups are perfect for those who wish to connect with other members within their areas of interest and/or practice. Specialized practice groups can help you familiarize yourself for opportunities aligning with your registered dietitian passion(s) and enhance your job performance and likeability.

If going back to school to advance your education in a masters or doctorate degree is something you are considering, please revisit your passions. Maybe you are passionate about education, business and marketing, or public health. By advancing your career and choosing a speciality or advanced degree you are passionate about, you can reap professional benefits like being more marketable to future employers, developing your skillset and expanding your practice, ability to negotiate reason for a higher salary and become more invested in something you know you already love.

Here is some additional food for thought: According to a study by Accenture in 2013, consumer healthcare is close to a 500 billion dollar market and is expected to double in growth over the next five years with the majority of dollars spent and growth focusing on preventative Health and Wellness categories including nutrition. This is exactly why our profession is growing. We can and will create our own place in the industry and provide the demand for nutrition expertise. There is no need to be stuck in rut. There is no need to stay in a job you do not find purposeful. There is no reason not to stay true to your passion.

What would you do if you quit your job today?

In many recent discussions with colleagues and friends, this common question comes up: **"I want to do something different but really, what would I do?"**

If you are having these feelings it is time to dig deep. Think hard. Start a list if you need to. There is no reason to be dissatisfied with something you spend 40+ hours a week doing. You wouldn't sleep on an uncomfortable bed or wear shoes all day that hurt your feet. You would do the research, go to a store, test out beds, try on shoes and invest in your comfort. Think of the time and energy you put into this decision making. Your career needs the same, if not more attention.

Ultimately, when you ask yourself "I need a change, but what would I do?" you must realize the perfect job is not going to come to you. You have to put a little work into finding and cultivating opportunities for yourself. If you want it, have the passion for it, put the work in and never feel like you have worked a day in your life.

And maybe right now, at this very moment, being employed as a registered dietitian might not be your thing. Maybe you just need a break to reassess. There was a point in my career when I was working at the hospital in which I planned to take a sabbatical of my own. I thought it would be nice to be a barista in a coffee shop and take a few steps away from dietetics. It had nothing to do with nutrition, a hospital or taking home my work. It had everything to do with conversation, providing people a service that generally makes them happy and enjoying a bright atmosphere to work in. When I was exploring this option, I knew I could always re-invent my nutrition passion in another way. I was still passionate about nutrition and dietetics but being employed at the time, was wearing me down.

This is when I looked at my hobbies outside of my professional life.

During this time in my life, I was really into baking and reading. I would bake everything and anything and enjoyed reading fiction, so a light bulb went off when I was working on this planned professional break. I would work as a barista, but I would volunteer my time using my nutrition expertise. I would volunteer at the local elementary school (which was one block away from where I lived) by teaching mini-nutrition lessons a couple times a month and pick an evening out of the month in which I would bake healthier items for a local food pantry's meal service. Volunteering in something completely different but still using my registered dietitian brain was the perfect "vacation" break I needed at the time.

You do not need to be employed by an entity who requires your RD credentials to have a fulfilling career.

Volunteering can have an important impact on the health and wellness of all types of communities. By volunteering, you are offering up your expertise for those in need but you are also giving back to yourself. Volunteering can help reduce stress in your life, foster stronger self esteem, and help you develop the framework for living out your passion.

The most important thing to remember is to create your own story, tell your story and live out your passion in the way(s) it works the best for you. There is no time like the present to get excited about your professional future. There is no time like present to be working at a job that does not feel like work. There is no time like the present to MAKE IT HAPPEN. You are not too young; you are not too old. Your happiness and satisfaction should not be an option when you know deep down inside what you truly want to be when you grow up.

All change is hard at first, messy in the middle and gorgeous at the end.
- Robin Sharma, a self-help writer and leadership speaker.

Now What? Workfheet
Now What? Workfheet

Exercise #1: Create Your "Be the Face of Nutrition" Toolbox

1. **Get a professional headshot done**. They do not cost a lot and you can have them taken in different outfits and as many times as you want until you are happy with them. Capture your personality in the picture. Make sure the picture really represents what you look like and how you dress in real life. You want to be recognizable; it needs to look like the real you. Get a digital file, so you can use your headshots in all types of communication. Also, as time passes by, your looks change (for the better, of course), so keeping the photo current is important. I recommend a new headshot each year. If you have ever attended your state affiliate yearly meeting or the Food & Nutrition Expo from the Academy of Nutrition and Dietetics, professional head shots are usually available.

2. **Order business cards**. Get them with your photo on them. Business cards are an easy way to put yourself out there without being overbearing or spending a lot of money. I leave my business card in many different places with many different people. This is a fun example: I left my business card in a fishbowl at a local restaurant to be entered for a free lunch. I was chosen (yay food!), and there was an employee at this business who was just diagnosed with celiac disease and needed help. She had no idea where to go and thought I would be able to help her. Free food and a client? Win-win!

3. **Order thank you post-cards or notecards with your photo on it and contact information**. This is a great way to follow-up with people or groups you have worked with. Not only are you thanking them for their business and for choosing the expertise of a registered

dietitian, you are giving them a reason to contact you again. You become "their registered dietitian." People remember and appreciate personal touches of gratitude. Who doesn't love receiving actual mail?

Exercise #2: Look into Leadership

For more information and contacts for your state affiliate, visit www.eatrightpro.org/resource/membership/academy-groups/affiliate/state-affiliates

1. Contact the leader of the state affiliate and inquire about about districts. Districts are local groups in your state that are a part of your affiliate. It is a great place to start with leadership because the group resides where you live and usually has scheduled meetings throughout the year.

2. If you are currently active in your district and would like to take it to the next level, contact the President or President-Elect in your affiliate. These individuals are the ones who identify the leaders for their council.

3. Most affiliates have elected positions each year, also known as the board. If you would like to be considered for one of these positions, contact the Nominating Committee who seeks out candidates for open positions.

4. I would love for you to visit my affiliate website and get a feel for the wonderful leadership in my home state of Iowa: www.eatrightiowa.org

Exercise #3: Determine What You Want to Be When You Grow Up

1. **Do a job search.** There are thousands of them out there. Do not look at location, just focus on the jobs and the description. Mark those catching your interest the first time through. This first process might take a few days or weeks. You are doing this to get an idea of what makes you excited and interested about your profession. Also, this search will give you an idea of the variety of jobs that are out there. It is good to re-introduce yourself to what is happening right now in dietetics.

2. **Go back through the jobs you marked and reread them (again, do not pay attention to location).** Pick out keywords capturing your interest and write those down. Once you get through the jobs you marked, spend some time looking over the list of keywords. Visit the list each day for a couple of weeks to really absorb what you are interested in when it comes to a job. Pick out the top five keywords that repeatedly speak to you.

3. **Do a job search again.** Go back to the job search engine and type in each of the five keywords separately and view the results. Then add "dietitian nutritionist" to each of the keywords and search again.

   Do you see where I am going with this? Your sincere interests can match up with dietetics. Hopefully, there were a few jobs that have or had you considering looking into them further. I know, location has A LOT to do with where you choose to work. And maybe there isn't anything currently available matching your interests, but it does not mean you should stop looking. You now have YOUR criteria that will help you find a long-lasting career you love.

   If you want it bad enough, continue the search. This search may also give you ideas of how to create your own perfect position in your current zip code. Add your city or state to your keyword search. With this search, a specific registered dietitian job may not come up, but other like-minded businesses will. This is where you could be the registered dietitian they don't know they need and are looking for.

Conclusion

Now What?

A recipe has no soul, you as the cook must bring soul to the recipe.
- Thomas Keller, American chef, restaurateur, and cookbook writer.

I know I worked hard to get where I am today. I know I am loved by a tribe of people who have been with me every step of the way. I know I have given much opportunity in my professional life. I know I was meant to be a registered dietitian.

YOU are meant to be a Registered Dietitian.

You are meant to experience all of what this profession has to offer. You are meant for greatness. You are meant to do it "your way."

It is easy to travel lightly around many different things in our lives. We dabble in this, we experiment with that. We give a little, just enough to test the waters. At the end of the day, we really have two choices: be all in or get out. When you decide to be all in, you truly realize if that's where you want to be or if you're better off somewhere else. You owe it to yourself to know and half-assing is not the way to go. Give it all you have or maybe it is time to walk away.

Wherever you are along your registered dietitian journey, I hope you want to be there. I hope you are not going through the motions and you find it fulfilling and meaningful. I hope it is challenging and exciting. I hope it is positive and you are being supported. I hope it brings a smile to your face and graciously gives you joy. And if it isn't, I hope you are brave enough to recreate the registered dietitian life you have always wanted to live, not considering for a minute to walk away.

When you take a step back and look at what has happened and what is currently happening in your life, are you satisfied with it all?

Or do you deserve so much more? Maybe it is not about "deserving." Maybe it's about believing in "so much more." We do not deserve a thing in life, good or bad. We create our lives and we either let things continue the way they are or we make the decision to change them. Be the change in your life and you will recognize when you can have so much more.

I always remind myself that nothing is going to happen if I do not put in the appropriate time and dedication. It is all up to me how I want things in my life to turn out. If someone or something unexpectedly beautiful happens along the way, I know there is a reason. It does not make me work any less hard, but it perpetually continues the joy of being grateful. All of it. The good, the bad and the ugly. Keep putting the work in. Stay true to course. Stay grateful.

Some people confuse crazy with passionate.
Let me be clear, I am bat sh*% passionate.
- Anonymous

I embrace a little crazy on occasion and I embrace passion just a tad bit more. To be crazy passionate about something, keeps your soul alive and keeps you living a true and authentic life. You need to have this kind of passion for dietetics to keep your authenticity balanced and complete. There will always be options. Endless, tireless, and an unlimited amount of options for everything in life. But when you are always out searching and going through every option, you're possibly taking yourself away from what the true priorities are in your life. The biggest one being yourself and where your passion truly lies.

What exactly are you traveling this earth searching for?

Are you keeping yourself and your passion the priority?

Are you traveling away or traveling closer to what you already know and what you want in your life?

Are you waiting for something to happen without putting the work in?

Waiting for something great to happen without passion and purpose, you will get nowhere. When you wait, you worry, you over think and you miss opportunities. Being great and finding greatness is all about the effort you put forth, the opportunities you create, the life you are meant to live. No matter how small, how insignificant or common those opportunities may seem now, it's all about what you put in, give and create to make greatness live constantly in every part of your life. Don't you dare miss out on that. Make your life, every minute, every second, absolutely and completely great.

It is never too late to hit the reset button and it is never too late to write your own story. Do not ever stop asking yourself "now what?" By asking yourself this and by reading this book, you might find new life, inspiration and comfort along your registered dietitian journey.

We are connected, not only by our profession, but you are now part of my tribe. I am here for you along the journey in this crazy and exhilarating registered dietitian world, and I hope we find ourselves sipping on a cup of tea together, having a explorative conversation discussing our past, present and our future now whats?

I need friends who can handle my ingredients, from cherries to nuts.
- Anne Elizabeth, Registered Dietitian, Author
and Now What? Expert.

Always be mindful that every day is another day to grab the bull by the horns and make something out of it. No more wasting, regretting, feeling sorry or ungrateful for all the beauty there is in life. Right now, you get to have this moment and the many other amazing moments shaping your life. Some of them have been happy, heartbreaking, lesson learning and magical glimpses of the future and what can be.

I know I am not promised one second of my life, but I am so damn happy. Every second I have had along this journey has been mine, all mine.

This journey of being a registered dietitian has been pretty bad ass so far. I know whatever is to come is what I will make of it. I will go after it, no matter how far I have to go. And I know I will not be alone.

Cheers to passion, purpose, our story, and our journey!

Cheers to being pure magic, finding joy and being great always!

Cheers to being a registered dietitian and always asking ourselves, "Now what?"

Anne Elizabeth

What if I fall? Oh, but my darling, what if you fly?
- Erin Hanson, Australian Writer and Poet.

References

Fleishman - Hilard. *New National Marketing-to-Moms Study*. The Motherhood, 8 January 2013.
http://www.themotherhood.com/blog/survey-predicts-food-buying-habits/
10 May 2016.

Greenwald & Associates. *The 2015 Food & Health Survey: Consumer Attitudes Toward Food Safety, Nutrition and Health*.
International Food Information Council Foundation (IDIC) 8 May 2015.
http://www.foodinsight.org/2015-food-health-survey-consumer-research
10 April 2016.

Amidor, Toby. *Calling All Food Bloggers*. Today's Dietitian, June 2013.
www.todaysdietitian.com/newarchives/060113p22.shtml.
2 February 2015.

Beyer, Julie, Dobbins, Melissa Joy. *Claim the Spotlight! Beyond Traditional Media: Videos, Podcasting, and Self Publishing.* Academy of Nutrition and Dietetics: Food and Nutrition Conference & Expo, 4 October 2015.
http://www.starlibraries.com/fnce/session/2009/Claim-the-Spotlight-Beyond-Traditional-Media-Videos-Podcasts-and-Self-Publishing.
 11 July 2016.

Russell, Karen. *Modern Mentoring: The Good, The Bad and The Better.* TEDx Talks. 30 June 2011.
https://www.youtube.com/watch?v=SSZRtx8m3Z8
17 February 2014.

Academy eMentoring Program. Academy of Nutrition and Dietetics, 2016.
http://mentoring.eatright.org/public/page.cfm?id=20
3 May 2016.

Mehrabian, Albert.. *Silent messages: Implicit communication of emotions
and attitudes.* Wadsworth (currently distributed by Albert Mehrabian,
am@kaaj.com) 1981.
 http://www.kaaj.com/psych/smorder.html
16 July 2015.

State Affiliates. Academy of Nutrition and Dietetics, 2016.
http://www.eatrightpro.org/resource/membership/academy-groups/affiliat
es/state-affiliates.
5 May 2016.

Iowa Academy of Nutrition and Dietetics, 2016.
http://eatrightiowa.org.
5 May 2016.

Board Certified Specialist. Commission on Dietetic Registration, the
Credentialing Agency for the Academy of Nutrition and Dietetics, 2016.
https://www.cdrnet.org/certifications/board-certified-specialist and
https://www.cdrnet.org/board-certification-in-advanced-practice.
11 July 2016.

Certificate of Training in Weight Management. Commission on Dietetic
Registration, the Credentialing Agency for the Academy of Nutrition and
Dietetics, 2016.
https://www.cdrnet.org/weight-management/certificate-of-training-in-wei
ght-management
11 July 2016.

National Board of Nutrition of Nutrition Support Certification. American
Society for Parenteral and Enteral Nutrition, 2016.
http://www.nutritioncare.org/NBNSC/
11 July 2016.

Certification Information. National Certification Board for Diabetes
Educators, 2016.
http://www.ncbde.org/certification_info/
11 July 2016.

AADE Diabetes Prevention Program Lifestyle Coach Training. American
Association of Diabetes Educators, 2016.
https://www.diabeteseducator.org/practice/diabetes-prevention-program/l
ifestyle-coach-training
 11 July 2016.

Become a Certified Leap Therapist. Lifestyle and Eating Performance, Signet
Diagnostic, 2016.
http://certifiedleaptherapist.com/clt-training/
11 July 2016.

About Certification. Institute for Functional Medicine, 2016.
https://www.functionalmedicine.org/certification_program/About/
11 July 2016.

*Become an Integrative and Functional Nutrition Certified Practitioner
(IFNCP).* Integrative and Functional Nutrition Academy, 2016.
https://www.ifnacademy.com
26 July 2016.

*Integrative and Functional Medical Nutrition Therapy (IFMNT) for Health
Professionals.* Next Level Functional Nutrition, 2016.
http://nextlevelfunctionalnutrition.com
26 July 2016.

Foodservice Management Professional® (FMP®) Certification.
ManageFirst Program™. National Restaurant Association, 2016.
https://managefirst.restaurant.org/fmp/
11 July 2016.

Health Coach Certification. American Council on Exercise, 2016.
http://www.acefitness.org/fitness-certifications/health-coach-certification/
default.aspx.
11 July 2016.

Online Certificate of Training Programs. Academy of Nutrition and Dietetics,
2016.
http://www.eatrightpro.org/resource/career/professional-development/dis
tance-learning/online-learning
11 July 2016.

Dietetic Practice Groups. Academy of Nutrition and Dietetics, 2016.
http://www.eatrightpro.org/resources/membership/academy-groups/diete
tic-practice-groups
11 July 2016.

Baldwin, Whitney, Davis, Philip J., Stenstrand, Mikael. *The Changing Future
of Consumer Health.* Accenture. 2014.
https://www.accenture.com/us-en/~/media/Accenture/Conversion-Assets/
DotCom/Documents/Global/PDF/Industries_2/Accenture-Changing-Future-
of-Consumer-Health-High-Performance-Business-Study-2013-Update.pdf
3 March 2016.

About

Anne Elizabeth Cundiff, RD, LD, LSC, FAND

Don't be afraid to give up the good to go for the great.
- John D. Rockefeller

Anne Elizabeth Cundiff, RD, LD, LSC, FAND, is a nutrition expert and a retail registered dietitian for Hy-Vee, Inc. in Des Moines, Iowa. In this role, Anne has focused her nutrition expertise by obtaining the CDR Certificate of Training in Adult Weight Management in March 2003, completing her certificate in wellness coaching from Des Moines University in February 2009, and becoming certified as a Lifestyle Coach with the American Association of Diabetes Educators in February 2016. Anne's purpose is to meet clients where they are on their wellness journey and provide the most relevant information on all aspects of nutrition in and out of the grocery store through nutrition counseling, community and corporate wellness, wellness presentations and a variety of media outlets.

Anne graduated from Creighton University in Omaha, Nebraska, and attended Iowa State University for her dietetic internship. Prior to working with Hy-Vee, Anne was employed as a clinical dietitian, practicing her nutrition expertise at Creighton University Medical Center in Omaha, Nebraska, and shared her extensive nutrition knowledge with future registered dietitians, nurses and dental students as an adjunct professor with Iowa Western Community College in Council Bluffs, Iowa.

With more than 15 years of living her purpose and passion as a registered dietitian, she enjoys helping other registered dietitians find their purpose and passion. She is a member of the Iowa Academy of Nutrition and Dietetics serving as President, Marketing Chair, Media Spokesperson and the recipient of the 2013 Medallion Award and of the 2016 Outstanding Dietitian of the Year Award. Anne is grateful for her passions of writing, speaking, wellness and, of course, food. Her creative and inspirational outlet is her blog, *Nutritional Noshes.*

She is an award-winning blogger for the Academy of Nutrition and Dietetics Food & Nutrition Magazine Stone Soup Blog, an expert with Best Food Facts, a Nutrition Communicator with the Midwest Dairy Council and an RD Coach for the Meet the Challenge Program with the Academy of Nutrition and Dietetics Foundation. She is a daughter, a sister, a godmother, a horrible golfer, a BFF, and a skin-care-obsessed, music-loving and hardworking woman.

Connect with Anne on:

The Web: www.anneelizabethrd.com

Twitter: @AnneElizabethRD

Instagram: @AnneElizabethRD

iTunes / Podcasts: Conversations with Anne Elizabeth, RD